Modern Critical Interpretations

Samuel Taylor Coleridge's
The Rime of the
Ancient Mariner

Modern Critical Views

These and other titles in preparation

Modern Critical Interpretations

Samuel Taylor Coleridge's

The Rime of the Ancient Mariner

Edited and with an introduction by
Harold Bloom
Sterling Professor of the Humanities
Yale University

Chelsea House Publishers ◇ *1986*
NEW YORK ◇ NEW HAVEN ◇ PHILADELPHIA

© 1986 by Chelsea House Publishers, a division of Chelsea
House Educational Communications, Inc.
133 Christopher Street, New York, NY 10014
345 Whitney Avenue, New Haven, CT 06511
5014 West Chester Pike, Edgemont, PA 19028

Printed and bound in the United States of America

∞ The paper used in this publication meets the minimum
requirements of the American National Standard for
Permanence of Paper for Printed Library Materials,
Z39.48–1984.

Library of Congress Cataloging-in-Publication Data

Samuel Taylor Coleridge: the Rime of the ancient mariner.
  (Modern critical interpretations)
  Bibliography: p.
  Includes index.
  1. Coleridge, Samuel Taylor, 1772–1834. Rime of the
ancient mariner—Addresses, essays, lectures.
I. Bloom, Harold. II. Series.
PR4479.S26 1986   821'.7   86-2576
ISBN 0-87754-734-3 (alk. paper)

Contents

Editor's Note

This volume gathers together the best criticism devoted to Coleridge's *The Rime of the Ancient Mariner* during the past quarter century, arranged in the order of its original publication. I am grateful to Hillary Kelleher for her aid in editing this book.

The introduction argues that the *Rime* is a parable of the Primary Imagination, rather than an allegory or ironic narrative of the Secondary Imagination. This argument is directed implicitly against Robert Penn Warren's powerful and influential New Critical reading of the poem, which perhaps neglects its daemonic aspect in order to do justice to its Christian symbolism. Warren's interpretation is developed in Elliott B. Gose, Jr.'s analysis of "symbolic language" in the poem, an analysis that sees Coleridge as remote, for once, from "our relation to Wordsworthian nature."

An enormous contrast is provided by William Empson, who refuses to regard the poem as "an allegory in favor of redemption by torment," and wants it to be instead a tribute to Western European maritime expansion. Charmingly outrageous, Empson quite seriously extends his polemic against the Christianizing of imaginative literature. The equally distinguished critic, Geoffrey H. Hartman, characteristically reads the *Rime* as a study in the problematics of representation, a justification of the highly self-conscious Romantic self.

In Warren Stevenson's essay, Coleridge's supernatural ballad is judged as a "miniature epic," on the Romantic theme of the western voyage. Very different is the witty exegesis of Frances Ferguson, who centers upon "the deluded reader," and so upon the tropes of perspectivism which constitute a poem that may portray redemption, or even perhaps "a deluded capitulation to the devil." These complexities of perspectivism enter also into Lawrence Lipking's account of the poem's beautiful marginal gloss, which he interprets as part of a divided text and sets against the poem itself.

Leslie Brisman's exegesis intricately traces Coleridge's defense against both ancestral and successor voices, thus finding in the poem an ironic narrative of the quest to escape influence. Finally, the psychoanalytic reading by Camille Paglia daringly suggests that the Ancient Mariner is an insufficient sexual being, so that the *Rime* becomes an introduction to *Christabel*, whose sexual personae are more fully developed. In some sense, her speculations return us full circle to the introduction, with its melancholy judgment that the Mariner is trapped in a repetition-compulsion.

Introduction

Poetry (and potentially its criticism) alone of all human talk need not be reductive. Coleridge in *The Ancient Mariner* tells a story that relates itself clearly to a major Romantic archetype, the Wanderer, the man with the mark of Cain, or the mocker of Christ, who must expiate in a perpetual cycle of guilt and suffering, and whose torment is in excess of its usually obscure object and source. This archetype figures in Blake and in Keats but is more basic to Wordsworth and Clare and Beddoes. In Coleridge, Byron, and Shelley it becomes something more, a personal myth so consuming that we hardly know whether to seek it first in the life or in the work.

The Ancient Mariner is in the tradition of the stories of Cain and of the Wandering Jew, but it does not reduce to them. It is a late manifestation of the Gothic Revival, and its first version is clearly to be related to the ballad of *The Wandering Jew* in Percy's *Reliques,* but its historical sources also tend to mislead us when we attempt to describe it in its own terms, which is the business of criticism.

The Ancient Mariner, bright-eyed and compulsive, is a haunter of wedding feasts, and in a grim way he is the chanter of a prothalamium. Yet he does not address himself to bride or groom but to a gallant who is the bridegroom's next of kin. His story means most, he implies, when it is juxtaposed with the special joy of the wedding celebration, but it is not relevant to those being joined by a sacrament. Its proper audience is an unwilling one; its function is monitory. The message can only be relayed from a lurker at the threshold to a prospective sharer of the feast.

The world of the Mariner's voyage is purely visionary; the ship is driven by a storm toward the South Pole and into a realm simpler and more drastic than the natural world of experience. Into a sea of ice, where no living thing was to be seen, through the snow fog there comes suddenly a great sea bird, the albatross. An albatross, with its wingspread of eleven feet and its length of some three and a half feet, and its white color, is a startling phenomenon in itself, and its great power of flight can easily betoken the generosity of nature. Whatever its source, and Coleridge leaves this mysterious, the poem's albatross comes to the mariners as a free gift. They hail it in God's name as if it were human; they domesticate it with their food, which it has never eaten before; they play with it as if it were child or pet. Very directly they associate it with their luck, for now the ice splits, a south wind springs up, and they start the journey northward back to the ordinary world. The poem's first great event is suddenly placed before us; without apparent premeditation or conscious motive, the narrator murders the albatross.

The murder is a gratuitous act, but then so is the initial appearance of the bird. There is a tradition of seemingly motiveless malevolence that goes from Shakespeare's Iago (whom Coleridge saw as a tragic poet, manipulating men rather than words) and Milton's Satan to the protagonists of Poe, Melville, and Dostoevsky, and that appears in Gide, Camus, and other recent writers. The tradition begins with the demonic (tinged with Prometheanism), moves (in the later nineteenth century) into a vitalism crossed by the social image of man in revolt, and climaxes (in our own time) in a violence that yet confirms individual existence and so averts an absolute despair of self. Coleridge's mariner belongs to this tradition whose dark ancestors include Cain, the Wandering Jew, and the Judas whose act of betrayal is portrayed as a desperate assertion of freedom by Wilde, Yeats, and D. H. Lawrence.

This tradition's common denominator is that of a desperate assertion of self and a craving for a heightened sense of identity. This is what the Mariner brings about for himself, in a death-in-life purgatorial fashion; for his companions he brings only a terrible death and a mechanical life-in-death following his own partial redemption.

Several influential modern readings of *The Ancient Mariner* have attempted to baptize the poem by importing into it the notion of Original Sin and the myth of the Fall. But the Mariner is neither disobedient in his dire action nor altered in nature by its first effects. There is nothing in him to suggest the depravity of the natural heart, nor is the slaying of an albatross at all an adequate symbol of a lapse that demands expression in the language of theology. Coleridge in his *Table Talk* (May 31, 1830) felt the poem was already too overtly moral (thinking of the pious conclusion) and said of it:

> It ought to have had no more moral than the Arabian Nights'
> tale of the merchant's sitting down to eat dates by the side of a
> well, and throwing the shells aside, and lo! a genie starts up,

and says he *must* kill the aforesaid merchant *because* one of the date shells had, it seems, put out the eye of the genie's son.

The Ancient Mariner seems to have just this peculiar moral logic; you shoot an albatross quite casually, as you might throw aside a date shell. The tradition of the gratuitous crime also characterizes itself by its emphasis on the casual as opposed to the causal. Lafcadio in *Les Caves du Vatican*, just before performing his crime without a motive, says, "It's not so much about events that I'm curious, as about myself." Lafcadio and the Mariner are not (in advance) concerned about what ensues from an act; the act for each becomes a bracketed phenomenon, *pure act*, detached from motivation or consequences, and existent in itself. But the Mariner learns not to bracket, and the poem would have us learn, not where to throw our date shells, nor to love all creatures great and small, but to connect all phenomena, acts and things, in the fluid dissolve of the imagination:

> O! the one Life within us and abroad,
> Which meets all motion and becomes its soul

Frequently noted by critics is the extraordinary passivity of the Mariner. Wordsworth first said that the Mariner "does not act, but is continually acted upon." Not only does the Mariner rarely act (he shoots once, drinks his own blood once, so as to cry out that he has seen a sail, and blesses once), but usually he expresses no reaction to events. Most of the strong emotional and moral statements in the poem are in Coleridge's frequently beautiful marginal prose. The Mariner is merely an accurate observer, not a man of any sensibility. Despite the wonder and terror of what befalls him, he does not reach a height of emotional expression until part 4 of the poem, and then is driven to it, fittingly, by *solitude*. Alone with the dead men, and surrounded by the slime of subhuman life, he wakens first into agony of soul, then into a sense of contrast between the human and what is "beneath" it in the scale of being, and finally into a startled awareness of unexpected beauty. The crisis comes with moonrise on the seventh night of his lonely ordeal. The marginal prose meets the crisis with a beauty of expression which seems to touch at the limits of art:

> In his loneliness and fixedness he yearneth towards the journeying Moon, and the stars that still sojourn, yet still move onward; and every where the blue sky belongs to them, and is their appointed rest, and their native country and their own natural homes, which they enter unannounced, as lords that are certainly expected and yet there is a silent joy at their arrival.

He can be saved only by translating this yearning from the moon and stars to what envelops his own loneliness and fixedness, by naturalizing himself in his surroundings and finding a joy that will intimate the one life he shares with the creatures of the great deep. The finest stanzas in the poem trace his transference of love from the moon and stars to "God's creatures of the great calm":

> The moving Moon went up the sky,
> And no where did abide:
> Softly she was going up,
> And a star or two beside—
>
> Her beams bemocked the sultry main,
> Like April hoar-frost spread;
> But where the ship's huge shadow lay,
> The charmèd water burnt alway
> A still and awful red.
>
> Beyond the shadow of the ship,
> I watched the water-snakes:
> They moved in tracks of shining white,
> And when they reared, the elfish light
> Fell off in hoary flakes.

The moon's beams *bemock* the ocean, because upon that rotting and still torrid surface (the moon is just rising and the heat of the tropical sun yet abides) an appearance of "April hoar-frost" is now spread. The light given by the water snakes is called elfish and is said to fall off "in hoary flakes." Moonlight and hoarfrost are an imaginative unity at the close of "Frost at Midnight"; they give and take light, to and from one another, and the light, like the fair luminous mist in "Dejection," is emblematic both of creative joy and of the One Life of the phenomenal universe.

The Mariner now sees the beauty and happiness of what he had characterized, not inaccurately, as slime:

> O happy living things! no tongue
> Their beauty might declare:
> A spring of love gushed from my heart,
> And I blessed them unaware:
> Sure my kind saint took pity on me,
> And I blessed them unaware.

> The self-same moment I could pray;
> And from my neck so free
> The Albatross fell off, and sank
> Like lead into the sea.

His consciousness remains passive; he blesses them "unaware." As a sacramental moment this is unique, even in Romantic poetry. A less than ordinary man, never before alive to the sacramental vision of Nature as life, joy, love, suddenly declares the most elemental forms of life in Nature to be joyous and deserving of his affection. The slimy sea serpents are nearly as formless as the chaos Coleridge is to dread in his late poems of "Positive Negation," "Limbo," and "Ne Plus Ultra." Yet these creatures have color and beauty, they are alive, and "everything that lives is holy," as Blake insisted. At this, its climactic point, *The Ancient Mariner* is the most vital and imaginative achievement of Coleridge's poetry. Here, for once, he places complete trust in his Imagination, and it cannot fail him.

The Ancient Mariner is not, like "Kubla Khan," a poem about poetry. The shaping spirit, or Secondary Imagination, is not its theme, though recently critics have tried for such a reading. The Mariner's failure, and his subsequent salvation, is one of the Primary Imagination, "the repetition in the finite mind of the eternal act of creation in the infinite I AM." God looked upon His Creation and saw that it was good. The Mariner has now first learned to repeat in his very finite mind this eternal act of perception and creation. This awakening certainly does not bring the whole soul of this man into activity; the Mariner does not learn to order his experience so as first to balance and then be free of it. He falls victim to it, and its eternal verbal repetition becomes his obsession. Had the Mariner been a poet, he could have written the Rime he incarnates. He has seen the truth, but the truth does not set him free. He returns to life as a mere fundamentalist of the Primary Imagination, endlessly repeating the story of his own salvation and the one moral in it that he can understand:

> He prayeth best, who loveth best
> All things both great and small;
> For the dear God who loveth us,
> He made and loveth all.

The other moral is less simple but quite as elemental. Coleridge has written the poem as an alternative reaction to the Mariner's experience, for that experience of purgation through love of the One Life is his own. The higher Imagination shapes truth; the lower merely takes it, through Nature, from the Shaping Spirit of God. The poem celebrates the continued power of creative joy in its creator. But the poem also foreshadows the eventual fate of its creator, when the activity of the whole soul will yield to torpor. Coleridge as theologian and philosopher found more willing auditors than the Mariner did, but his quest came to duplicate that of his creation.

Coleridge and the Luminous Gloom: An Analysis of the "Symbolical Language" in *The Rime of the Ancient Mariner*

Elliott B. Gose, Jr.

Speaking of the "plan of the 'Lyrical Ballads' " in chapter 14 of his *Biographia Literaria*, Coleridge pointed out that while Wordsworth was to deal with "the wonders of the world before us," he himself was to try to connect the human truth of "our inward nature" with the "shadows of imagination." The fruitfulness of this connection is evidenced by *The Ancient Mariner*; its aesthetic basis was analyzed by Coleridge at a later date: "The romantic poetry," he decided, appeals "to the imagination rather than to the senses and to the reason as contemplating our inward nature, the working of the passions in their most retired recesses." By "exciting our internal emotions," the poet "acquires the right and privilege of using time and space as they exist in the imagination, obedient only to the laws which the imagination acts by." Philosophically, Coleridge's transcendentalism is obviously responsible for this assertion of the superiority of the mind over nature; he had remarked its psychological basis as early as 1805:

> In looking at objects of Nature while I am thinking, as at yonder moon dim-glimmering through the dewy window-pane, I seem rather to be seeking, as it were *asking* for, a symbolical language, for something within me that already and for ever exists, than observing anything new. Even when that latter is the case, yet still I have always an obscure feeling as if that new phenomenon

From *PMLA* 75, no. 3 (June 1960). © 1960 by the Modern Language Association of America.

were the dim awakening of a forgotten or hidden truth of my
inner nature.

(Anima Poetae)

In view of statements such as these, the critic is justified in asking whether
The Ancient Mariner does not employ a language more figurative than literal
to tell of events more inward than outward.

I

In recent years there have been several attempts to explain the symbolism in *The Ancient Mariner*. The two most important published interpretations are Robert Penn Warren's well-known 1946 essay and George
Herbert Clarke's lesser-known and less ambitious "Certain Symbols in *The
Rime of the Ancient Mariner*" (*Queen's Quarterly*, February 1933). As Warren
sees it, the poem has two themes, first "the theme of sacramental vision
or the theme of the 'One Life' " and second "the theme of the imagination."
The first centers on the killing of the albatross. In the second, "the moonlight equates with the 'modifying colours of the imagination,' " while the
sun "is the light of that 'mere reflective faculty' that 'partook of Death' ";
"in the poem the good events take place under the aegis of the moon, the
bad events under that of the sun." Clarke's approach is similar to Warren's,
though simpler and different in emphasis. As he sees it, "the Sun (with the
Polar Spirit and the first Voice) is conceived in Coleridge's imagination as
suggesting the stern, just, masculine, punitive side of the nature of God;
and . . . the Moon (with the Hermit and the Second Voice) normally
symbolizes the gentle, feminine redemptive side," As the word "normally"
suggests, any thorough treatment of these symbols must account for their
ambivalence in a more comprehensive way than either Clarke or Warren
do.

According to Warren's interpretation, the voyage taken by the Mariner
is a mental journey from conventional daytime thoughts to the land of
imagination. Faced with this "land of ice, and of fearful sounds where no
living thing was to be seen" (Gloss), the crew is terrified. But their fear is
abated and the ice splits before them after the appearance of the Albatross;
"as if it had been a Christian soul, we hailed it in God's name." Because
they accept it on these terms, the Mariner is wrong to kill it, as are his
fellows to judge the act solely by its value to them. Their crime is at once
slighter and more mundane than the Mariner's; therefore, they suffer death
at the Pacific equator, while he undergoes the harsher punishment of life

in death. This situation is what Warren refers to when he talks of the theme of "sacramental vision or . . . the 'One Life,' " presumably taking the last phrase from "The Eolian Harp" which speaks of "the one Life within us and abroad" (l. 26). But this pantheistic belief becomes sacramental only when God is brought in, and Warren does bring Him in with his claim that the Mariner commits the original sin when he kills the bird. I would support Warren's interpretation, citing St. Augustine's definition of original sin: "The soul abandons Him to whom it ought to cleave as its end, and becomes a kind of end to itself." The Mariner's act is as much an attempt to negate God's principles as to set up his own, but the results of that act demonstrate his inability to function once he separates himself from God. For such a crime it is fitting punishment that the Mariner is left alone, surrounded by the soulless bodies of his friends, reminders of what he had repudiated in killing the Albatross.

So far we have followed Warren's hypothesis that in killing the Albatross the Mariner separates himself from a Christian God—and certainly the poem is filled with Christian trappings. It begins with a church wedding and ends with an admonition to pray in church. In between we have mention of Christ, Mary Queen, Heaven, Spirits blest, Him who died on the cross, penance, Dear Lord in Heaven, a holy hermit, and shrieving. Finally, Coleridge indicates that the Albatross is important to the theme of the poem because it symbolizes a Christian soul. And along with these Christian concepts and figures, we find a symbolic identification of God with the sun: "Nor dim nor red, like God's own head, / The glorious Sun uprist." Ironically, Warren's emphasis on Christianity leads away from his interpretation of the sun as symbolic of the "mere reflective faculty" and to a broader application of Clarke's connection of the sun and God. This connection has a long and honorable history in Western culture, including Plato, Plotinus, and Augustine, to mention only three of the earliest and most relevant writers. The qualities of the sun which Coleridge used in making it a symbol for God are discussed in the next two sections.

II

The most important scene in the poem is the blessing scene at the end of part 4. Although it has been mentioned by most critics, only John Livingston Lowes has analyzed it minutely. And whereas he was interested in the sources of its images and how they were combined, we shall be interested in their meaning. The moon appears to dominate the scene.

Her beams bemocked the sultry main,
Like April hoar-frost spread:
But where the ship's huge shadow lay,
The charmed water burnt alway
A still and awful red.

Beyond the shadow of the ship,
I watched the water-snakes;
They moved in tracks of shining white,
And when they reared, the elfish light
Fell off in hoary flakes.

Within the shadow of the ship
I watched their rich attire:
Blue, glossy green, and velvet black,
They coiled and swam; and every track
Was a flash of golden fire.

O happy living things! no tongue
Their beauty might declare:
A spring of love gushed from my heart,
And I blessed them unaware:
Sure my kind saint took pity on me,
And I blessed them unaware.

The beams of the moon are "like April *hoar-frost*," white and cold coming together as they did at the end of part 1 when the moon first appeared and when the gloss spoke of "snow-fog." These qualities are transferred to the water snakes in the next stanza: "shining *white*" and "*hoary* flakes." Equally important, however, is a contrast in these stanzas. The moonbeams *mock* "the *sultry* main" away from the ship, "*But* where the ship's huge shadow lay, the charmed water *burnt* alway a still and awful *red*." This contrast between the white, cold light of the moon, and the red, burning color in the shade is emphasized by a deliberate further contrast in the next two stanzas. The one connecting the water-snakes with white and hoary begins "*Beyond* the shadow of the ship." The next one begins "*Within* the shadow of the ship," and gives an entirely different description of the snakes: Their "every track was a *flash* of *golden fire*." And it is following this sight that the mariner is able to bless them. His conversion then does *not* take place because of the light cast on the snakes by the moon—comments by Warren, Clarke, and a host of other critics to the contrary notwithstanding.

Rather, the snakes are transformed by the red fiery light of the shadowed water. The importance of temperature becomes evident when we remember that the Mariner had earlier been put under the control of the "Night-mare life-in-death . . . / Who thicks men's blood with cold," after which "fear at my heart, as at a cup, My life-blood seemed to sip." And later,

> I looked to heaven, and tried to pray;
> But or ever a prayer had gusht,
> A wicked whisper came, and made
> My heart as dry as dust.

This state changes when "A spring of love gushed from my heart / And I blessed them unaware." Love warms the blood and is thus the immediate means of his spiritual rebirth.

Love and warmth have an important source outside the Mariner. We are told that he is allowed to bless the snakes by his "kind saint," God's emissary. Remembering that God is symbolized in the poem by the sun, we can not only connect the saint with Him but also relate the "golden fire" with the sun, and appreciate both the imagistic and dialectic impact of the Mariner's conversion. The analogy of God's love affecting man as the sun's warmth affects nature was well established in Coleridge's mind, as is clear from the ending of "Religious Musings" (1794–96):

> In ministeries of heart-stirring song,
> And aye on Meditation's heaven-ward wing
> Soaring aloft I breathe in empyreal air
> Of Love, omnific, omnipresent Love,
> Whose day-spring rises glorious in my soul
> As the great Sun, when he his influence
> Sheds on the frost-bound waters—The glad stream
> Flows to the ray and warbles as it flows

Another way of phrasing the analogy in these lines is, Sun is to glad stream freed of cold as Love is to glad self freed of doubt. The passage is expressive of that joy which was so important to Coleridge (as we find in "Dejection: An Ode") and which is hinted at in the "*April* hoar-frost" dissipated at the end of part 4 to be replaced by the joyful dream which begins part 5.

III

But having established God the Sun as the source of life and love and joy, we have still not exhausted its symbolic import. In addition to its heat, the sun has color; it is "bloody" at the Pacific equator and afterward the shaded water is an "awful red." The same color is present when the Mariner returns to land, a scene very similar in imagery to the blessing scene.

> The rock shone bright, the kirk no less,
> That stands above the rock:
> The moonlight steeped in silentness
> The steady weathercock.
>
> And the bay was white with silent light,
> Till rising from the same,
> Full many shapes, that shadows were,
> In crimson colours came.
>
> A little distance from the prow
> Those crimson shadows were:
> I turned my eyes upon the deck—
> Oh, Christ! what saw I there!
>
> Each corse lay flat, lifeless and flat,
> And, by the holy rood!
> A man all light, a seraph man,
> On every corse there stood.

In the original version of the poem (in the *Lyrical Ballads*) Coleridge included four stanzas immediately preceding these and emphasizing "dark-red shadows."

> (The moonlight bay was white all o'er,
> Til rising from the same,
> Full many shapes that shadows were,
> Like as of torches came.
>
> A little distance from the prow
> Those dark-red shadows were;
> But soon I saw that my own flesh
> Was red as in a glare.

> I turn'd my head in fear and dread,
> And by the holy rood,
> The bodies had advanc'd, and now
> Before the mast they stood.
>
> They lifted up their stiff right arms,
> They held them strait and tight;
> And each right-arm burnt like a torch,
> A torch that's borne upright.
> Their stony eye-balls glitter'd on
> In the red and smoky light.)

Just as in the moonlit scene at the end of part 4 the Mariner was about to reestablish harmony with God, so in this moonlit scene halfway through part 6 he is about to reestablish harmony with society, but both important changes are preceded by a vision of red in the shadow *out* of the moonlight. The importance of red imagistically in the poem indicates a philosophic importance which Coleridge later expressed in prose: "The interpenetration of Light and Shade in the highest unity, or the identity of Light and Shadow is RED, colour [preeminently] in positive energy." The positive energy of the blood helps explain why Coleridge emphasizes it in describing the mariner's conversion. Red is also the color of the sun when it appears at the Pacific equator as "the bloody sun" of the Old Testament God of wrath demanding retribution for the Mariner's crime. But in the New Testament, blood is important as the sacrifice Christ made to save man from original sin and bring him back into God's grace. In this way Christ as the embodiment of the eternal in the temporal represents the penetration of the light in the dark. ("I am come a light into the world, that whosoever believeth on me should not abide in darkness" [John 12. 46].) Similarly, the Ancient Mariner is saved by the immersion of God's light in the shades of this world, which explains why the sun is not physically present in either of the moonlit scenes discussed, though it does figure in the imagery of both. In the blessing scene we are told that the "water *burnt*" and the snakes' "every track was a flash of golden *fire*." And in the harbor scene, as the discarded lines make clear, the spirits are on fire: "each right-arm burnt like a torch." These spirits, of course, are the angelic troop previously connected with God the Sun.

I would emphasize, however, that before the Mariner sees the spirits, he is made aware of their presence in a situation analogous to that in the earlier blessing scene: "A little distance from the prow those crimson shadows were." In both these key transition scenes, then, the Mariner becomes aware of the divine by seeing it in the shadows of this world, "the interpenetration of Light and Shade," and in both cases that interpenetration results in "the highest unity, or the identity of Light and Shadow . . . RED." What we have is not the result of any absolute logic or metaphysic; it represents simply the imagistic dialectic of Coleridge's mind. But the process of investing images with meaning was one which he felt was characteristic of all minds, as shown by his assertion in the *Biographia Literaria* that "an IDEA, in the highest sense of that word, cannot be conveyed but by a symbol." The source of the symbolic value of the particular image we are concerned with can be inferred from a phrase in Coleridge's Notebook Number Five (dated 3–7 November 1799 by Kathleen Coburn in her edition of the notebooks): "The sunny mist, the luminous gloom of Plato—" Besides being a concentrated image for the penetration of the light in the dark which we have found in two key scenes in *The Ancient Mariner*, "the luminous gloom" also has an important connection with Coleridge's philosophic development. The year before he began writing *The Ancient Mariner*, he finished a more overtly philosophic poem, "The Destiny of Nations," (1796):

> For what is Freedom, but the unfettered use
> Of all the powers which God for use had given:
> But chiefly this with holiest habitude
>
> (l. 15)
>
> Of constant Faith, him First, him Last to view
>
> (l. 15a)
>
> Through meaner powers and secondary things
> Effulgent, as through clouds that veil his blaze.
> For all that meets the bodily sense I deem
> Symbolical, one mighty alphabet
> For infant minds; and we in this low world
> Placed with our backs to bright Reality,
> That we may learn with young unwounded ken
> Things from their shadows. Know thyself my soul!

The individual sees God by looking at the shadow, an analogy that bears a close resemblance to Plato's myth of the cave, which Coleridge evidently had in mind when he attributed "the luminous gloom" to Plato. But where Plato scorns the shadows which constitute our world of the senses, calling them inferior copies of the ideal, Coleridge tells us "all that meets the bodily sense I deem / Symbolical, one mighty alphabet" by which to see God.

The real affinity of Coleridge's images, then, is with later Platonic thought. This is especially true of "thy sunny mist" which appears in the foregoing passage as God the life-giving sun Whom it is better to see "Through meaner powers and secondary things / Effulgent as through clouds that veil his blaze."

The sun does not appear south of the equator, in the land of ice and snow, until the first stanza of part 2, at which point the ship has left the known Atlantic and entered the unknown Pacific. "The Sun now rose upon the right," and is "hid in mist," causing the crew to chide the Mariner. Soon, however, it rises "Nor dim, nor red, like God's own head," and they praise his deed. But according to Coleridge in "The Destiny of Nations," the proper way to see God is through mists "that veil his blaze." Seeing him directly is a foretaste of the vengeance which soon comes: "All in a hot and copper sky / The bloody sun at noon / Right up above the mast did stand."

But awful as is God's vengeance, the excess of his presence, even worse comes with the appearance of the Spectre ship which cuts the mariners off from the sun.

> That strange ship drove suddenly
> Betwixt us and the Sun.
>
> And straight the Sun was flecked with bars,
> (Heaven's Mother send us grace!)
> As if through a dungeon grate he peered
> With broad and burning face.

Further, the sun is forced to set after the spectre woman wins the dice game. God, the source of life, punishment, and redemption, is replaced by another force, not just black death (which is a negation of God's light), but the Nightmare life-in-death who wins the Mariner. She is obviously outside the Christian hierarchy and is connected with a whole strand of non-Christian figures, incidents, and images in the poem. The Polar region, for instance, is presided over by the Polar Spirit, which is of a different order from the angelic spirits, being specifically labelled as outside the Christian framework by the gloss: "A spirit had followed them; one of the invisible inhabitants of this planet, neither departed souls nor angels; concerning whom the learned Jew, Josephus, and the Platonic Constantinopolitan, Michael Psellus may be consulted. They are very numerous, and there is no climate or element without one or more."

Where the sun is connected with man's immortal soul, the moon is

connected with the one life or mutable nature, as is clear from two stanzas
at the beginning of part 6.

> Still as a slave before his lord,
> The ocean hath no blast;
> His great bright eye most silently
> Up to the Moon is cast—
>
> If he may know which way to go;
> For she guides him smooth or grim.
> See, brother, see! how graciously
> She looketh down on him.

Smooth or grim. As Warren has pointed out, the storm in part 1 is connected
with the moon, as is that in part 5. But in addition to the storms, the moon
has a grim persona, which appears in part 3, the grimmest section of the
poem. The death ship, we have seen, cuts the mariners off from God, just
as utter darkness negates the sun. If dark death takes the mariners from
sun-life, what function is filled by the "Night-mare life-in-death"? "*Her*
lips were red, *her* looks were free, her locks were yellow as gold: her skin
was white as leprosy, . . . she . . . thicks men's blood with cold." That
she is the alter ego of the moon is indicated by the white cold connected
with her. The vengeance of the moon is to put the Mariner into a state in
which he is incapable of love. In fact nature becomes to him what it is to
"the poor, *loveless* ever-anxious crowd" in "Dejection: An Ode"—an "*in-
animate, cold* world."

In his review of *The Monk* (*Critical Review*, Feb. 1797), Coleridge
praises "the tale of the bleeding nun" as "truly terrific," and calls "the
character of Matilda . . . the author's masterpiece. It is, indeed, exquisitely
imagined, and as exquisitely supported." Looking forward to the Nightmare life-in-death and to Geraldine, we can understand Coleridge's appreciation of Lewis' two demon women. The influence of the bleeding nun
on the "Spectre-Woman" in *The Ancient Mariner* is especially worth remarking. Rather than develop the parallel in detail, however, I would like
to emphasize the image Lewis has his narrator use when he describes the
nun leaving him. "The charm now ceased to operate; the blood which had
been frozen in my veins rushed back to my heart with violence; I uttered
a deep groan, and sunk lifeless upon my pillow." That Lewis' frequent
connection of cold with the demonic struck Coleridge as appropriate is
indicated by his singling out the scene in which "blue fires . . . increase the
cold of the cavern."

Coleridge also approves Lewis' use of "the burning cross on the forehead of the Wandering Jew." But despite the undoubted influence of *The Monk* on Coleridge, his objections to it should be recorded, especially since they neatly distinguish it from real literature. The following is obviously a variation on the theme which Coleridge later developed to justify his supernatural poems:

> The romance-writer possesses an unlimited power over situations; but he must scrupulously make his characters act in congruity with them. . . . The extent of the powers that may exist, we can never ascertain; and therefore we feel no great difficulty in yielding a temporary belief to any, the strangest, situation of *things*. But that situation once conceived, how beings like ourselves would feel and act in it, our own feelings sufficiently instruct us; and we instantly reject the clumsy fiction that does not harmonise with them.

When on the return voyage the ship again reaches the Atlantic equator, it is stopped. The gloss tells us that "the Polar Spirit's fellow-daemons, the invisible inhabitants of the element, take part in his wrong; and two of them relate, one to the other, that penance long and heavy for the Ancient Mariner hath been accorded to the Polar Spirit, who returneth southward." In other words, though God has been satisfied by the Mariner's blessing of the water snakes, the representatives of this world demand additional penance.

We have already noted that in part 4 the light of the moon makes an important contrast to the luminous dark with which the Mariner's conversion is associated. The imagery at the end of the poem brings in the moonlight again, indicating that the compulsion the Mariner feels to tell his tale is associated with the moon. In the next to last stanza we are told, "The Mariner, whose eye is *bright*, whose beard with age is *hoar*, is gone." As Clarke has pointed out, the Mariner's eye connects him with the crew who curse him with their eyes by "the star-dogged moon." We may also remember two stanzas already quoted in which the ocean's "great bright eye most silently / Up to the Moon is cast." The Mariner's life-long penance is having to act like a "grey-beard loon." Yet his listeners "cannot choose but hear," a tribute to the power of the moon and lunacy, as was clear in some lines included in the original version of the poem: "Marinere! thou has thy will: / For that, which comes out of thine eye, doth make / My body and soul to be still."

The Mariner had regained harmony with God first and decisively in the blessing scene, in images which were reiterated in the harbor scene. But not until he mixes with the mortals of this earth is he enabled to do bodily penance for his violation of the one life. In 1802 Coleridge wrote in a letter to Sotheby, "Nature has her proper interest, and he will know what it is who believes and feels that everything has a life of its own, and that we are all *One Life*." The word *proper* indicates that by 1802 (as in *The Ancient Mariner* itself) Coleridge's pantheism is subordinate to his transcendentalism. More simply, nature is subordinate to God: philosophically and poetically, man's relation to nature is subject to time, whereas the relation of his soul to God is timeless. The absolute nature of this second relation means it can be fixed once and for all, as I feel it is in the blessing scene. The relative nature of the first relation explains why it must be reaffirmed throughout the Mariner's life. But in truth the Mariner tells us little of our relation to Wordsworthian nature, to wind, sea, sun, and moon. Our premise has been that his tale deals with no literal geographical voyage. Rather it is emblematic of the Romantic urge to explore the eternal soul and the temporal emotions. The voyage was Coleridge's, as it becomes the reader's: plunged like all men into the mist and gloom of life on this planet, he sought to comprehend the lifegiving source which called up that mist, to appreciate the luminosity which informed that gloom. *The Ancient Mariner* is the finest fruit of that labor.

*T*he Ancient Mariner

William Empson

Most people receive the impact of the poem when young, and to that extent it is not at the mercy of critics; but critics have done a good deal to spoil it for them when older, usually while claiming to point out its merits (as I am doing myself, I must remember). There is often a question whether you should read into a poem the beliefs and interests of the author when he wrote or instead allow it the traditional meanings imposed by his society; and I think wrong answers have been given here both ways round. The *Mariner* appeals to a proud national tradition and evokes a major historical event, the maritime expansion of the Western Europeans; but a number of recent critics have expressed relief that the fanciful reverie is so free from politics. On the other hand, most of them take for granted that it is an allegory in favour of redemption by torment, the central tradition of Christianity; not liking perhaps to say in front of the children that Coleridge was a Unitarian at the time, that is, had cut himself off from most white-collar employment because he disapproved of this plan for redemption. To make the poem Christian one must argue that the Mariner committed a real crime, and this has afforded many critics a steep but direct path to the wild heights of Pecksniffery which are their spiritual home. Even Humphry House, who wrote well (*Coleridge*, 1953) about what Coleridge meant in saying that the poem had too much of the moral, and should have been like an anecdote which he recalled from the Arabian Nights—even he went on to call shooting the Albatross "a ghastly violation of a great sanctity, at least as bad as

From *Critical Quarterly* 6, no. 4 (Winter 1964). © 1964 by Sir William Empson.

a murder." A student at Sheffield wrote in an essay for me that she would have hanged the Mariner from the yardarm with her own hands; I had to warn her that the External Examiner would consider this to be in the wrong tone of voice, but she was expressing the orthodox modern view. I think it does the poem a lot of harm.

II

Coleridge at this time called himself a Christian, meaning that he revered the moral teaching of Jesus; he was also fond of saying that ordinary Christians were materialists, because they believed that matter could exist without a soul (as a teakettle for example); but this is polemical or witty language. Most of the people he met would not have said he was a Christian till he was beaten down into agreeing that the crucifixion was the means of redemption. In 1798, the year after writing the poem, he was offered a post as a Unitarian minister, but said that the congregation must be free to reject him after he had explained why he could not administer the Lord's Supper (the rite most intimately connected with human sacrifice). He came of a clerical family and the unction was natural to him, also he thought it a duty not to encourage atheism, so that his objections to Christianity were left obscure; but they were binding upon himself. Whether absurdly or not, he was determined not to be seduced into supporting beliefs which he disapproved; he would not have done it even in a ballad. As to politics, his group of friends in Devonshire had told him to shut up; there was a real police terror, though it so happened that nobody we have heard of was among those hanged, and a spy had reported to the Home Office "a set of violent Democrats" in Devonshire. Maybe Coleridge felt contentedly that he was still helping the cause, because he might be read by the censor, when he said in his letters, "I have snapped my baby trumpet of sedition." In a letter of August 1797, not long before starting the poem, he is trying to induce one of the set to seclude from the police the agitator Thelwall:

> If the day of darkness and tempest should come, it is most probable that the influence of T. would be very great on the lower classes. It may therefore prove of no mean utility to the cause of Truth and Humanity, that he had spent some years in a society where his natural impetuousity had been disciplined into patience, and the slow energies of a calculating spirit.

No wonder he despised the Government for suspecting him, as he made these statesmanlike plans; but the duty of discretion was not at all likely to exclude politics from his mind.

He wanted a theme of guilt and remorse and had been writing on Cain before Wordsworth gave him the brief anecdote about an albatross in Shelvock's *Voyage*; this suited him as he had been reading earlier travellers' reports, chiefly for a series of Odes on the four elements. Also he positively wanted to write on superstition. A basic impulse of the Romantics was to escape from the eighteenth century, their enlightened parents in fact, so as to experience if only through history and travel books the variety of the world. Superstitions were found everywhere on these journeys, and a Romantic would often adopt one; but Coleridge (as is obvious in the first draft of the *Mariner*) was quite ready to laugh at olde-worlde sensationalism. He needed superstition in poems for a philosophical purpose; to examine the psychological function which gave it this universal appeal. Wordsworth was himself writing poetry about his immediate experience but agreed that Coleridge should contribute poems with:

> the persons and characters supernatural, or at least romantic, yet
> so as to transfer from our inward nature a human interest and
> a semblance of truth sufficient to procure for these shadows of
> imagination that willing suspension of disbelief for the moment
> which constitutes poetic faith.

The famous phrase was thus coined to deal with a special effort of historical imagination; he was to show

> the dramatic truth of such emotions as would naturally accom-
> pany such situations, supposing them real. And real in this sense
> they have been to every human being who, from whatever
> source of delusion, has at any time believed himself under su-
> pernatural agency.

But we are not to suppose that Coleridge liked superstitions, or wanted to encourage them; in a letter of July 1802, which can be unusually frank as it is to a brother Unitarian, he says of possession by spirits:

> not only did it imply frightful corruption in the great article of
> all religion, the moral attributes of God; but it must needs have
> had a bad effect and an anti-social influence on the intercourse
> between man and man . . . Yet so far are these Exorcists from
> being condemned by Christ that their innocence is cited by him
> to prove his own. St. Paul directly asserts the existence of wicked
> spirits swarming in the air.

Such beliefs in fact are rather like madness; the reality behind a superstition of fourteenth-century sailors may well be the same "fact of mind" as the private neurosis of Coleridge himself. The works of the Romantics, I think, are merely tiresome unless one recognises that they are based upon assumptions of this sort; the authors were courageous and generous-minded, and right in thinking they had a new world to describe.

The great merit of *The Road to Xanadu* was in showing that Coleridge had read widely in the ships' captains' reports, and that whole verses of the poem were word-for-word quotations from their prose; no wonder it is so much better than what he had written before—the naked strength of the language is behind the *Mariner*, as if English had been evolved solely to write this one poem. Regarded as a summing-up of the maritime expansion, to make it turn on a superstition was no more than just; the sailors had dared their great journeys while notoriously fearing still greater perils than the real ones. We are told that this crew is the first to enter the Pacific and we see them invent a superstition about an albatross; probably they were the first to see an albatross, but as often in legends the name of the creature is taken for granted. The weather had become less unhelpful when it appeared, so the crew at first blame the Mariner for shooting it, but as soon as the sun comes out they say he was right—they are only sure that the incident was numinous enough to have a magical effect. (In a splendid illustration by Gustav Doré the sailors huddle, white with rime among burgeoning shapeless icicles, all gaping at a bird which estimates them quizzically like the Dodo in *Alice*). The Mariner seems to imply a mild criticism of the crew for this rapid change of mind, and the author cannot have expected it to recommend the superstition to his readers. The Mariner, however, is struck down by guilt as by the Furies, and I have no wish to weaken the obvious violence of the effect; I only say that we are intended to balance it with an equally obvious reflection: "how free from guilt he is, according to our own beliefs." It took a sad lack of sturdiness in the modern world, I think, to obscure this point altogether.

The Mariner says nothing about why he shot the bird, partly because he now regards the action as beyond palliation, and the author wants a feeling of mystery. But we can get some indications from the first text. The storm had prevented revictualling:

> For days and weeks it played us freaks:

and by the time the Albatross came what victual was left had become nauseating:

> The Mariners gave it biscuit-worms.

Nobody who had been reading travellers' reports in bulk could doubt the motive of the Mariner after that; he shot it for food. All good explorers try out new sources of food; it is part of their scientific aspect, which gives them the dignity of Faust; and the darker Albatross mentioned in the anecdote of Shelvocke, which is just small enough to be hung round a man's neck, does, I am told, make a tolerable soup which would help to keep off scurvy. Probably this soup was made and drunk, so that only the externals of the Albatross were hung round the Mariner's neck later on; it would be easier to do. The Polar Spirit has then some excuse for killing the whole crew, and the text when carefully examined does not say that they invented the superstition against killing it as soon as it was killed. (I do not believe that there were two hundred of them; Coleridge or the Mariner invents this number to heighten the drama of their all dying at once.) Coleridge did not disapprove of eating flesh, though he ate little of it unless invited to dinner; he revered all life, vegetables included. (Advanced thought had simplified and hardened by the next generation, when Shelley was a vegetarian.) He would thus have no temptation to suppress the thought of food. Take the philanthropist Nansen; all teams such as his team had a schedule for eating the husky dogs who pulled the sledges, so that each time a sledge became empty, as the men and dogs ate the food on the sledges, there were no husky dogs to pull this useless sledge. I bet all those dogs loved Nansen like crazy. Anyhow, even granting that the Mariner deserved to be killed for killing the Albatross, all the rest of the crew did not deserve to be killed even more.

I am not denying that Coleridge said the Mariner had committed a crime; he said it in the second edition, while removing a lot of archaisms. He had come to realise that the poem deserved more solemn treatment than he had thought at first (maybe they laughed heartily on that walking-tour, sharing in a parody of the fashion for archaic ballads); but there was a more pressing reason. Wordsworth was very sore at the reviews of *Lyrical Ballads*, which had jeered at his prosiness; he showed an unreasonable inclination to blame Coleridge, who as usual was far too ready to kiss the rod. He offered to suppress his poem, so Wordsworth claimed afterwards that his fatherly encouragement had induced Coleridge to make it presentable. Such was how he came to cut out the excellent technicality "broad as a weft upon the left," which could have been explained at once in a footnote, and cut out some good though sensational bits of description; this caused some horrible discords in the sound as at ll. 372–73, "a quite tune. / Till noon we quietly sailed on," wrecking the exquisite harmony which the sound has all through the first version. The facetious archaisms urgently needed removing, but we pay a heavy price for it. Well then, the *biscuit-worms* and

the internal rhyme *freaks-weeks* (evidence of a long period without revictualling) were cut out for being ridiculous, not because the author had
decided to hush up the food shortage. He also altered the brief "Argument"
introducing the poem. Instead of "How a Ship . . . was driven by storms"
(reaching the Antarctic and the Pacific) "and of the strange things that befell;
and in what manner the Ancyent Marinere came back to his own country"
(1798), it says "how the Ancient Mariner cruelly and in contempt of the
laws of hospitality killed a Seabird and how he was followed by many and
strange judgements; and in what manner . . ." (1800). This was omitted
altogether in 1802 and the frequent subsequent editions, chiefly no doubt
because having an Argument at all came to seem tiresomely olde-worlde,
but also perhaps because Coleridge did not care to explain his fable. However, the marginal glosses, added at any time before 1817, give the same
explanation; "And lo! the Albatross proveth a bird of good omen." . . .
"The Ancient Mariner inhospitably killeth the pious bird of good omen."
To call it a "pious bird" must be intended as a mild parsonical joke, an
aside to relieve the boredom of the parents who overhear the children being
taught not to pull poor pussy's tail. The Antarctic is notoriously inhospitable, and its Spirit causes all the trouble; in most houses a guest would be
allowed to eat the available meat rather than starve to death. Coleridge was
trying to make his poem more acceptable by plugging the moral archly.
Still, he was not altering the story, and would not think he was altering
the interpretation. The poem itself says, or the Mariner before recovering
from a fit hears a voice in the air say:

> The spirit that bideth by himself
> In the land of mist and snow,
> He loved the bird that loved the man
> Who shot him with his bow.

From the first, this was intended as a powerful kick at prosy-minded readers
such as myself; and yet the rotund music depends on a distinction between
the man and the animal so basic that one takes *who*, the other *that*. The
Spirit is not inherently either good or bad, merely wilful, and a reader is
free to decide that it treated the men wrongly.

The young Coleridge who wrote the poem, I don't deny, had strong
impulses to agree with the Spirit; probably if he had heard about the ex-
termination of the Dodo he, too, would have recommended the yardarm.
The orthodox Coleridge who made comments long after was inclined to
laugh off this flouting of the rights of man over animals. But they both
thought the childishness of the moral was an actual recommendation, since

children unlike ourselves have not been corrupted by the world—they are "blest seers." In any case, the Mariner at the stage of his life when we meet him is being helped by magic to express a revelation—he can tell it in any language, recognising at a sight a man who needs to be told it, and the Wedding-Guest was sadder for knowing it, as well as wiser. What else can it have been but that killing the Albatross was a crime?

III

The poems that Coleridge had been writing just before make rather clearer how his mind had been moving. The terrors of Nature, he explains in "Religious Musings" (1794), were planned by God to awake the spirit of primitive man:

> What mists dim-floating of idolatry
> Split and misshaped the omnipresent Sire:
> And first by Terror, Mercy's startling prelude,
> Uncharmed the spirit spell-bound with earthly lusts.
> Till of its nobler nature it 'gan feel
> Dim recollections, and thence soared to hope

The typical "idol" was Moloch; "idolatry" means thinking God more malignant than he is, so the argument lets Coleridge believe that God is acting on a good plan though he sends earthquakes. (If you believe in an omnipotent God you have to admit that he sometimes chooses to act cruelly, however much you deny that he was specially satisfied by the crucifixion). But only primitive man needed teaching by terror; Coleridge holds out against believing that we need it ourselves. Even so, it is clear from "The Destiny of Nations" (1796) that men were still primitive in the time of Joan of Arc. The Mariner was also medieval, and I think we are expected to retain a certain superiority to him. He has received an almost blinding revelation, but we need not be sure that he knows how to interpret it. The author might indeed modestly disclaim having had the revelation himself; but I think he felt intimately and confusingly involved. The wicked whisper that kept the Mariner from praying must I think be "God is unjust to me"; it comes soon after the line, later expunged, saying that Christ would take no pity on him; but much of the poem is concerned to deny this idea energetically. Then again, the question whether you can love the slimy creatures would be bound up in his mind with the question whether you can love their Creator; and are they perhaps in some metaphysical sense a nightmare of your own? Such are the ideas that would be at the back of his mind when composing, though I do not mean that he deliberately worked them in.

IV

What then did one find, reading in bulk the reports of the European maritime expansion, which made it suitable for the Mariner to be struck down by guilt? Surely the answer is plain once the question is asked; they reek of guilt. Indeed Columbus himself, returning to Europe in the first triumph of discovery, when he sent a cutter racing ahead with the good news to Ferdinand and Isabella, lamented that the Caribbeans were so innocent, unsuspicious, and doomed. It may fairly be answered that this is unusual in a ship's captain; as a rule, what is startling in his narrative is the absence of any sense of guilt. A bit translated from the Portuguese struck me as good prose owing to its earnest piety;

> Then might you see mothers forsaking their children and husbands their wives, each striving to escape as best he could. Some drowned themselves in the water; others sought to escape by hiding under their huts; others stowed their children among the seaweed, where our men found them afterwards, hoping they would escape notice. And at last our Lord God, who giveth a reward to every good deed, willed that for the toil they had undergone in his service they should that day obtain victory over their enemies, as well as payment for all their labour and expense; for they took captive of those Negroes, what with men, women, and children, 165, besides those that perished and were killed.
>
> (*The Colonial Era*, H. Aptheker, 1960)

"What *use* was their religion if it did not tell them that this was wrong?"— such was the way it would appear to Coleridge, who boasted to correspondents around this time that he did not examine religious doctrines as a mere arguer but always in the light of their practical effects. Also he had been considering what useful steps an antislavery man could take; boycotting sugar appeared to be ineffective. Charles James Fox took advantage of a brief interval of power to abolish the slave trade in 1805, not long after the poem was written, and common opinion seems to have thought this overdue. The only actual superstition about albatrosses, it has turned out, was that they were ships' captains who had been drowned passing the Cape of Good Hope; perhaps then the story means "The explorers did not realise that the natives were human." One still meets this legend in print, and

Coleridge might come across it; but I have not found any case of it in the reports. The Terra del Fuegans were thought to be devils, not animals; and anyway to be classed as human gave a creature no protection. Thus it would not be right to say that the Albatross was a "symbol" of the ill-treated natives, but the terrible cry "I didn't know it was wrong when I did it" belongs somehow naturally to the whole setup of the exploring ship.

I became conscious of this around 1951 in Communist Peking. Sardar Pannikar, the Indian Ambassador, needed books; if you had been sent a book, not to hand it on would be cruelty, so I proferred *The Enchaf èd Flood* by W. H. Auden. Next time we met (I should explain that my wife and I were fortunate in being among the few residents the non–Communist diplomats might still invite) he growled out that it was all spoof. I said Auden had proved his case, because the English, French and Spanish Romantics all treated the sea in the way he described, but the Germans, having still no empire, didn't; the force of the argument lay in the negative control test. He reeled off quotations from the epics of three Indian languages to show that the sea is always the great sweet mother, to the poets. But that was Auden's point, I said, only the poets of the maritime empires did it. "Then they weren't really poets," he said, leaving me convinced that Auden had made an important discovery about *The Ancient Mariner*. Probably he reflected, though I did not, that India in the time of the poets he had quoted enjoyed a maritime empire extending to Bali and Indochina. Still, I can't really think it vulgar of the Europeans to be Faustian. The effect on literature of their maritime empires was to make the explorer a symbol of scientific discovery, upon which the ships themselves had depended, thence of intellectual adventure in general, and at last for the highest event in ethics, the moral discovery, which gets a man called a traitor by his own society. The Victorians continued to give a good deal of rope to a serious traveller; the *Art of Travel* by Sir Francis Galton (1855) says in its opening sentence that every traveller must be prepared to take the law into his own hands. Auden says:

> The Ancient Mariner and his ship represent the small but persisting class of mental adventurers . . . From the social point of view, these spirited adventurers are criminals; they disturb the social order and they imply a criticism of the accepted round of life; they are self-appointed outcasts . . . The Mariner escapes from his isolation by the enlargement of his sympathies in the manner least expected and he is allowed to return to common life . . . But he is still the marked man, the outcast, the

Wandering Jew, the victim of his own thought. Further, although he has been judged by society, he has the reward of the courage that propels the mental adventurer; that of arresting and disturbing and teaching those who have had no such experiences.

Rather too cozy perhaps but very central. This is what the poem is traditionally about; as it would still be if Coleridge did not discover the meaning till after he had written and then ratted on it as fast as he could.

V

But the poem was from the start more anchored the poet than that, and none of the changes he made are really alien to it. He was himself a martyr to neurotic guilt, feeling guilty without believing he had good reason for it; *The Ancient Mariner* is the first and best study of that mental condition. Such is the reason why he couldn't finish any of his books; "My sickness has left me" he wrote to Longmans (1801):

> in a state of mind, which is scarcely possible for me to explain to you—one feature of it is an extreme disgust which I feel at every perusal of my own productions, and which makes it exceedingly painful to me not only to revise them, but I may truly add, even to look on the paper on which they were written.

Many authors have felt like this, but to explain it to one's publisher is a heroic exercise of the Romantics' principle of self-expression. Coleridge usually just says he feels fear, and then shows by the example that he is afraid of being told that he has done wrong, or more usually that he has neglected a duty. He used laudanum to quiet this condition, and no doubt made it worse, but the condition was there beforehand. "The Pains of Sleep" (1803) gives a splendid description of his nightmares:

> But yesternight I prayed aloud
> In anguish and in agony,
> Upstarting from the feverish crowd
> Of shapes and thoughts that tortured me;
> A lurid light, a trampling throng,
> Sense of intolerable wrong,
> And whom I scorned, those only strong!

Deeds to be hid which were not hid,
Which all confused I could not know
Whether I suffered, or I did;
For all seemed guilt, remorse, or woe,
My own or others still the same,
Life-stifling fear, soul-stifling shame.

Such punishments, I said, were due
To natures deepliest stained with sin,
For aye entempesting anew
The unfathomable hell within,
The horror of their deeds to view,
To know and loathe, yet wish and do!

Such griefs with such men well agree,
But wherefore, wherefore fall on me?
To be beloved is all I need,
And whom I love, I love indeed.

In January 1805, he wrote in a notebook (*Inquiring Spirit*, Kathleen Coburn):

It is a most instructive part of my life, the fact, that I have always been preyed on by some Dread, and perhaps all my faulty actions have been the consequence of some Dread or other on my mind, from fear of Pain, or Shame, not from prospect of Pleasure. So in my childhood and Boyhood the horror of being detected with a Sore head . . . then a shortlived Fit of Fears from sex, then horror of *Duns*, and a state of struggling with madness from an incapability of hoping that I should be able to marry Mary Evans . . . Then . . . my marriage, constant dread in my mind respecting Mrs. Coleridge's temper, &c . . . since then every error I have committed has been the immediate effect of the Dread of those most shocking bad dreams—anything to prevent them.

This mental state, in which the sufferer from guilt does not admit he has sinned, was what Coleridge was likely to want to express in the poem, because it was so familiar and such a burden to him; and such is what his fable does express—in the mind of an unsophisticated reader, now as then, the Mariner does not deserve his sufferings. Modern critics must therefore be evading the real point of the poem when they so eagerly invent proofs that he did deserve them. You may answer that the author himself was too

ready with pathetic excuses, though really he deserved the punishment he got, so probably he is trying to delude us about the Mariner. But his views on Nature make him prone to blame the Mariner more than the expected reader would, and this saves the author from suspicion; the ambiguity of judgement heightens the effect. It was a splendid invention to kill all the Mariner's comrades and leave him alive with their dead eyes still cursing him, because he is then forced to blame himself more than we feel he deserves. They have died because he shot the Albatross, though he could not have guessed that the Spirit would use them as weapons to torment him. Also they have died because he called a ship to help them, biting his arm to be able to do it; this was a phantom ship containing Death, but he could not have known. After the gods had done him this injustice, he would not show good feeling or good taste if he did not overblame himself to an almost lunatic degree. Such, I think, is the evident point of this main part of the story.

Mr. D. W. Harding, in an article for *Scrutiny* during 1941, now available in his *Language into Words*, described the psychological background of *The Ancient Mariner*. I wasn't seeing the magazine then, and did not find a reference to the article till after drafting this piece; but he and W. H. Auden hold the priorities for the "inside" and the "outside" of the poem.

Coleridge found that walks in hilly scenery could do a good deal to palliate neurotic guilt; and this was the main basis in experience for the doctrine of the healing power of Nature through Imagination. Wordsworth in *The Prelude* describes his nightmares about revolutionary Paris in a fine passage very near to "The Pains of Sleep"; they had the experience independently, I expect, and then told one another about it. Coleridge's idea of a walk was a good deal: thirty miles over rough country he seems to have thought normal, as a young man, whatever he was saying about his bowels. There is an aside in one of his letters, perhaps the only time when he made an excuse which was more impressive than he realised. He could not have done what he has promised, he is saying as usual, because he has had a complication of illness, owing to crossing a pass in Westmoreland during a storm; and perhaps, it occurs to him, he may be told that he should have turned back; but this would be impossible to him, as it is not his habit: "I never once in my whole life turned back in fear of the weather" (*Letters*, 1802). We have long been told he was self-indulgent and weak-willed, and I now hear him called fubsy, but the trouble was that he was a compulsive character, who stuck to a line once adopted with appalling persistency. The reason why he had read everything was that he was a compulsive reader, who dared not stop; rather than open a letter from his wife, he would read straight on all through Purchas's *Pilgrims*. Schoolmasters are familiar with the type, which either does well or fails badly.

He thus expected Nature to be a bit rough; his everyday approach to her was rather like that of the explorer. The fundamental revelation granted to the Mariner, somewhat obscured by his compulsive technique of total recall, was granted to Coleridge himself about five years later and described in a letter to Sara Hutchinson:

> I began to suspect that I ought not to go on; but then unfortunately though I could with ease drop down a smooth Rock of 7 foot high, I could not *climb* it, so go on I must; and on I went. The next 3 drops were not half a foot, at least not a foot, more than my own height, but every drop increased the Palsy of my limbs. I shook all over, Heaven knows without the least influence of Fear. And now I had only two more to drop down—to return was impossible—but of these two the first was tremendous, it was twice my own height, and the Ledge at the bottom was exceedingly narrow (so) that if I dropt down upon it I must of necessity have fallen backwards and of course killed myself. My limbs were all in a tremble. I lay upon my Back to rest myself, and was beginning according to my custom to laugh at myself for a Madman, when the sight of the crags above me on each side, and the impetuous Clouds just over them, posting so luridly and so rapidly to northward, overawed me. I lay in a state of almost prophetic Trance and Delight and blessed God aloud for the powers of Reason and the Will, which remaining no Danger can overpower us! O God, I exclaimed aloud, how calm, how blessed I am now. I know not how to proceed, how to return, but I am calm and fearless and confident. If this reality were a Dream, if I were asleep, what agonies had I suffered! What screams! When the Reason and the Will are away, what remains to us but Darkness and Dimness and a bewildering Shame, and a Pain that is utterly Lord over us, or fantastic Pleasure that draws the Soul along swimming through the air in many shapes, even as a flight of Starlings in a Wind.—I arose, and looking down saw at the bottom a heap of Stones which had fallen abroad and rendered the narrow Ledge on which they had been piled doubly dangerous. At the bottom of the third Rock that I dropt from, I met a dead Sheep quite rotten. This heap of stones, I guessed, and have since found that I guessed aright, had been

piled up by the Shepherd to enable him to climb up and free the
poor Creature, whom he had observed to be crag-fast, but seeing
nothing but rock over rock, he had desisted and gone for help
and meanwhile the poor Creature had fallen down and killed
itself. As I was looking at these I glanced my eye to the left,
and observed that the Rock was rent from top to bottom. I
measured the breadth of the Rent, and found that there was no
danger of may being wedged in, so I put my knapsack round
to my side, and slipped down as between walls, without any
danger or difficulty.

There is a briefer record in his Notebook (August 1802):

pass along Scafell precipices; and came to one place where I
thought I could descend, and get upon the low ridge that was
between Scafell and Bowfell, and look down upon the wild
savage, savage head of Eskdale. Good Heavens! What a climb!
dropping from precipices and at last should have been crag-fast
but for the chasm.

—also a less attractive reference in a letter of 9th August: "Hartley is almost
ill with transport at my Scafell expedition." Poor little Hartley was not
then quite six years old, and far too much a wind-harp for Father to blow
upon; one can see how hard Father had puffed. But he might well be pleased;
he had just written "Dejection" and a series of letters about the pain of
losing his poetic genius, and now the thing had actually happened. There
is no sign of the vanity of an author—it does not occur to him that he has
enacted the Mariner; what has happened is far more important—the theory
about Nature has been proved true.

In his dealings with other people, Coleridge was too inclined to kiss
the rod and then shuffle out of reach of it: he deeply distrusted open conflict
or resistance. His passiveness before Nature here ("I bear pain with a woman's fortitude" he writes often) is rather the same, but it feels unaffectedly
grand (the style is like Defoe), and a modern climber would readily believe
that it saved his life. When in a tight place one should collect oneself and
not get rattled; otherwise he would have died like the sheep. Many climbers
would also recommend appreciation of the scenery, as a help in keeping
one's nerve at such a time; and this almost amounts to saying "Delight in
Nature when terrible gives one strength to control it." Coleridge of course
went further, believing that such delight marked an intuitive sympathy

with the natural objects by an act of Imagination (very remote from making up a poem), and therefore restored the individual to a proper relation to the universe.

The Active Universe by H. W. Piper (1962) shows that the view of Nature held by the earlier Romantics, however strange, was in line with "the current scientific orthodoxy." Contemporary reviews of poems by Wordsworth and Coleridge regularly explained what was new in their philosophy; pantheism was familiar enough, even in Pope, but the new poets combined it with animism, the belief in various kinds of Spirits which had been formative for Renaissance science. Thus they believed

> that the world-soul would be found in each material object and that, through the imagination, a real communication was pos-sible between man and the forms of nature.

Coleridge and Shelley both believed this, but Coleridge (thinks Mr. Piper) was dependent as a poet on a personal relation with Nature in some way that Shelley was not. It is clear at any rate that the Mariner did not need to be a criminal before he could acquire a revelation of this kind.

VI

We should now be equipped to reconsider the "moral" of the poem, "He prayeth best, that loveth best / All things both great and small." I would do wrong to belittle the moral "Don't pull poor pussy's tail," which needs to be taught to children; but Coleridge came to feel, like many of his readers, that it forms an inadequate conclusion to so much lightning and despair. What the Mariner had achieved was love of almost intolerable creatures, products of Nature when particularly inhospitable. I said in my *Some Versions of Pastoral* that Coleridge "insisted in the margin by giving the same name to both" that the creatures by which he was at first most disgusted were the same as those which he eventually blessed unawares for their beauty, so that they became his salvation. I still think this a fair point, but the engineering of the poet is more radical and complex. To call both of them "creatures of the calm" does not prove them identical but helps to suggest it; when Coleridge wrote these marginal notes he continued to encourage a suggestion already made in the text. When the ship reaches the equator in the Pacific "the Albatross begins to be avenged"; the sailors are dumb with drought, and

> The very deeps did rot; O Christ;
> That ever this should be!
> Yea, slimy things did crawl with legs
> Upon the slimy sea.
>
> (l. 125)

The water looked like petrol spilt on a motor road (next verse). More than a hundred lines packed with incident follow before these details are recalled, so we do not easily notice that the legs are omitted. The crew deduce from a dream that a Spirit is avenging the Albatross, so they hang the remains of it round the Mariner's neck. Delirium is probable by the time the skeleton ship appears to him—nothing definitely supernatural has occurred before. The unreasonable quality of supernatural justice is plugged home by the game of dice. Death wins the others, but life-in-death the Mariner; his condition when we meet him is a life in death, and Coleridge made play with the term again to describe his own life in his "Epitaph." That sailors are often victims of women when they strike land is a standard reflection, and the grand description of the prostitute White Goddess is entirely fitting for the "outside," though for the "inside" all it can mean is that the innocent Coleridge had been badgered by Southey into marrying a scold. An incurable syphilitic, unable to seek honourable love because he would give the beloved the disease which yet allows him to linger on, would strike Coleridge as an eminent case of life in death, not unusual among retired sailors; and the disease had actually been brought by Columbus from America. The skin of the goddess is white as leprosy, which poets have often made a sort of literary alternative to syphilis. Mr. Christopher Ricks has pointed out to me that Coleridge in one of his letters (quoted by House), mentions fearing in a dream that the breath of a spectral prostitute would give him the disease, and one can see that a terror then so eminent would have to be present in his nest of secret terrors, though his morality and his passivity would alike make him fairly safe from it. So the White Goddess is needed both for the inside and the outside of the poem, but I think he uses her mainly as a conjuring device, to distract our minds while all those legs drop off. The spectral ship goes, the sailors all die, and now for the first time the marginal gloss says *creatures*. "He despiseth the creatures of the calm" (the term of course reminds you that God created them) is put against:

> The many men so beautiful
> And they all dead did lie;
> And a thousand thousand slimy things
> Lived on, and so did I.

> I looked upon the rotting sea
> And drew my eyes away;
> I looked upon the rotting deck
> And there the dead men lay.
>
> (l. 240)

Their eyes continue to curse him. (It is not only wonderfully good, but wonderfully like a real ballad.) The healing Moon comes up, making possible his act of atonement by showing the creatures in a better light, and they are now "water-snakes" (l. 275); the words insist upon, and the rhythm makes vivid, a beauty of movement very unlike the movement of things that crawl with legs. The spilt-petrol colours recur but now seem hallucinatingly beautiful. These colours and the words *rot* and *slimy* all recall the things with legs, and the confident rotund gloss "By the light of the Moon he beholdeth God's creatures of the great calm" feels to me like a pious refusal to recognise a well-known unpleasantness: maybe they still had legs when he "drew his eyes away," and maybe their legs just dropped off quickly when the Moon got up; this would have been a magical bit of luck for the Mariner, because obviously he couldn't have loved them if they were still crawly. But the matter is handled with great tact, as it needed to be, because in theory he had to be able to love any degree of crawliness whatever.

One might expect Coleridge, with his Ommjective and Summjective, to make the Mariner recognise the snakes as part of his own nature; but he keeps very clear of that. The snakes are absolutely other to him, like beings of another planet, and it is an alien part of his own mind which blesses them; he is astonished that the saving act has been performed. I do not think there is any traditional Christian parallel to this; the process is entirely unlike, though it may easily recall, the repentant saint punishing himself by kissing the leper's sores. The process indeed is exactly the other way up. The Mariner is astonished to find his inside admiring what his outside had thought disgusting but at once feels happy and thankful about it, so that his outside joins forces with his inside; naturally his life can now be saved, and as the readers have been made to share his nausea for the creatures they can grasp the heroic character of his spontaneous reversal. This also deals with an objection, first raised by Wordsworth, that the Mariner does not do enough to make him the hero of a poem. The motives of Wordsworth in this complaint are obscure, but I am afraid that whatever they were they must have been bad. He was just as much involved as Coleridge was, or H. G. Wells later on, in a middle-class antiheroic propaganda, justified up to a point—a feeling that aristocrats had patented the honour of a soldier so that ratting on it was a class duty for literary men. Though the Mariner does every possible action for the survival of himself and his fellows, he could never appear as a fighting man; in the same way, because the rest of the crew are always united in decision, this is the only eminent sea story which never uses the thrilling words *captain* and *mate*. As a Pantisocrat, Coleridge felt that a ship ought to be imagined as a democracy (and Kinglake in *Eothen* reports that a small enough Greek ship really was); but a kind of artisan courage, from one of the crew, he felt allowed to praise; and the Mariner is a striking case of it. We assume he is demanding water for all his comrades when he hails the skeleton ship, because, if he had been dying alone, he could not have raised the strength to bite his arm and suck the blood so as to soften his mouth enough to shout. I think Coleridge ought to have told Wordsworth to try doing this himself before calling the Mariner insufficiently heroic.

VII

Psychologists tell me that they do not recognise the term "neurotic guilt," which I have long heard used as of a familiar reality. For example, Dylan Thomas, with the dead earnestness which so often came as a surprise, told me it was curious he was such a martyr to attacks of neurotic guilt, as he led such an innocent life, but he found the only way to handle them was to hide in the country for a week or two, stopping drinking altogether, speaking to nobody, and so on. His meaning in using this term was clear; he felt struck down by guilt though by his own principles he had done no wrong; and it was easy to reflect that he had done wrong by the principles of the hostess of Fern Hill, his peasant aunt. A psychologist (as I understand) finds this trivial because it does not involve the mechanisms of the deep unconscious, and indeed it is more like "split personality"—one moral code goes on dragging against another. But it is the most prominent cause of mental upset among present-day educated people, and I think psychologists belittle it because they dislike admitting that there can be genuine rational disagreement about a moral question. There was nothing mad about Coleridge except a peculiarly severe conflict of this kind; he could not bear to rebuff the fundamental sympathies of his society and yet found that accepting the theology in which they were expressed, when he was beaten down to it, was a kind of suicide.

The schoolboy Coleridge would enjoy being praised for his cleverness, however pathetic the elder man made him appear, but decided that there was no future for him in scholarship, since all the white-collar jobs which it dangled before him required a profession of belief in what Voltaire had shown to be infamous. In his charity blue-coat gown, he explored London and found a shoemaker willing not only to take him as apprentice but also to come and tell the headmaster. The headmaster threw out the man and beat the child (for being an infidel), and Coleridge in later life amused himself by saying that this was the only just beating of all his beatings at school. He was right, I expect, to remember it as important; it had made him unable to emerge from his childish terrors. This boy sounds a great deal more vigorous and enterprising than the grown-up Coleridge. There were two or three further cases of "I didn't know it was wrong when I did it," but the pattern had been established. He ran into debt at college, so he later said, because when a man came and asked how to decorate his rooms he said "As you please, sir," supposing the cunning tradesman to be a college official; so he ran away and enlisted to save his family the money, but this only gave them the extra expense of buying him out. His disastrous marriage followed the pattern; Southey had told him it was the right thing to do. We have two descriptions, by himself and by a student friend, of his behaviour at Cambridge in a week before he failed an exam, and it is an effort to believe that both are true. The brilliant gaiety was achieved by "acting a part" with iron resolution; but perhaps the suicidal despair was a bit playboy as well. This romantic style of behaviour has become tiresomely familiar, but we should remember I think that Coleridge had a genuine reason for it; he did not believe the religion which was technically required of him, so there must eventually have been a showdown when he refused to take the oath for his degree.

He made a principle of not publicising his basic religious objection, and I have only found one place where it becomes clear. On 27th September, 1796, Charles Lamb, who had been a younger but intimate schoolfellow of Coleridge, wrote that his sister Mary Lamb in a fit of madness had killed their mother. "Thank God, I am very calm and composed, and able to do the best that remains to do. Write as religious a letter as possible . . ." Coleridge was unable to resist writing letters which were too religious (he was twenty-three; Lamb was twenty-one). The first reply of Lamb (October 3rd) begins with the words "Your letter was an inestimable treasure to me," but the next one grieves that Coleridge is not settling down to a serious course of life, and the third (October 24th) questions the doctrines that Coleridge has preached:

> Again, in your first fine consolatory epistle, you say, "you are a temporary sharer in human misery, that you may be an eternal partaker of the Divine Nature." What more than this do those

> men say who are for exalting the man Christ Jesus into the second
> person of an unknown Trinity?—men, whom you or I scruple
> not to call idolaters.

Presumably an idol, a Moloch, is a God who demands human sacrifices.
Lamb is objecting to the idea that suffering makes us better because God
enjoys it; also, he finds it bad taste for Coleridge to talk as if God has been
kind to arrange a disaster so as to make Lamb better. He is deeply concerned
to comfort his sister, so he finds it morally disgusting to be told to reflect
that he himself is being polished for Heaven; has her murder polished *her*
for Heaven? Indeed, I think the case is one which makes the unpleasantness
of Christian consolation especially prominent. But I must not claim that it
was obvious to Lamb; his letters here express deep submission to the arbitrary will of God, as when he says, near the start of his first reply to
Coleridge:

> My poor dear, dearest sister, the unhappy and unconscious in-
> strument of the Almighty's judgements on our house, is restored
> to her senses—to a dreadful sense and recollection.

He is in no mood to isolate himself from the religious sentiments of his
society. Only just of age, he has already had a period in an asylum, and
now the senile father, the mulish aunt, the greedy brother, and the sister
who, whatever her merits, was liable to turn back into a tiger at any
moment, all depend for their bread upon his earnings as a clerk; he is taking
care to preserve his sanity, and rather surprised at his success. They are
impressive letters, especially as they are so far from the usual line of en-
deavour of a Romantic; and I think they suggest that both the friends had
been more logical and definite in their revolt against Christian doctrine
while still at school. Lamb's other objections in this letter seem to be against
Coleridge's pantheism, not his backsliding into orthodox Christian torture-
worship. But the sentence he quotes is not pantheist; for example, the
Athanansian Creed speaks of "the taking of the manhood into God." Coleridge presumably accepted the rebuke, as he remained a Unitarian for about
six more years.

We can see how hard it was to surrender to Moloch in a letter to his
parson brother George (July 1802); he thinks he has invented a way to
make terms with the Establishment without actually conniving at its basic
infamy. He has come to believe, he says, in an

> original corruption of our nature, from which and from the
> consequences of which we may be redeemed by Christ, not as
> the Socinians say by his pure morals or excellent example merely,

but in a mysterious manner as an effect of his Crucifixion; and this I believe, not because I *understand* it, but because I *feel* that it is not only suitable to but needful for my nature and because I find it clearly revealed.

What he still cannot endure to say here is that the Father was satisfied by the Crucifixion; he would have called that, surely, as already quoted, "frightful corruption in the great article of all religions, the moral attributes of God" (the quotation at least shows that he was not too innocent to regard a theological question in that light). The process he was going through here was a frequent one, summarised with ghastly exactitude at the end of *1984*, in the pathetic delay of Winston Smith before gulping down last of all a somewhat disguised form of the doctrine "God loves torture." A later stage of the same struggle is recorded in what Coleridge called his "happiest effort in prose composition," the "Preface to Fire, Famine etc." (appendix 3 in the Oxford text of the *Poems*), first printed in 1817 but claiming to report a conversation probably held in 1803; it is a laboured piece of sophistry to the effect that seventeenth-century theologians did not really believe in Hell. When he returned from Malta (1806) he had become keen on arguing for the doctrine of the Trinity, and for ever after treated himself as an interesting moral invalid.

I may well be told that, as the defences of Coleridge against the religion were so inadequate, he could let it creep into *The Ancient Mariner*. There are indeed plenty of expressions of straightforward piety by the Mariner, as is historically correct. But Coleridge just then was enjoying his brief period of triumph, especially the triumph of finding a friend he could revere; he expects the religion to be easy enough to handle—technical difficulties will melt away when confronted with real vision, and the certainty of offering a real vision is the very tone of his voice and gleam of his eye. A recent book *The Enchanted Forest* (W. W. Beyer, 1962) gives an interesting sidelight. It shows that many of the details of the *Mariner* came from Wieland's verse romance *Oberon*, which Coleridge was translating from the German at the time (so he claimed in a letter). It might seem that this discovery refutes the Auden generalisation, but I do not think so; the only sea travel is in the Mediterranean. The hero, a vassal of Charlemagne, kills a son of Charlemagne in self-defence when ambushed treacherously on his way to Court; he can only be pardoned if he carries off and marries the caliph's daughter. So far he is trying to recover his due status; but halfway through the poem he commits a sin. The daemon Oberon has blessed his union with the Saracen princess but added that it must not be consummated till blessed by the Pope; while they are sailing to Rome this rule is broken (the lady seeing no need for it) and they are thrown overboard in a tempest for prolonged trials and sufferings. Mr. Beyer several times calls the temptation "provocative," evidently as a term of praise; I think he means that the lust of the reader is excited by the needless exasperation imposed on the characters. If so, he justifies, without meaning to, the behaviour of Coleridge, who never admitted his debt to *Oberon* but said in later life that "Wieland's subject was bad, and his thought often impure" (*Table Talk*, May 1811). This reaction must have come early, because Wordsworth in 1798, evidently relying on Coleridge's judgement, snubbed Klopstock by saying it was "unworthy of genius to make the interest of a long poem turn entirely upon animal gratification." A snuffy thing to say, but Coleridge really did find the theme somehow in bad taste. The Romantics often anticipate the Victorians, who felt that a gentleman should know how to avoid the indecent struggles for virginity recorded of the saints. Wieland had his free-thinking side but was prepared to screw as much drama as possible out of Christian chastity; and this is already vulgar because insincere. The Victorians were right, I think, so far as they were tacitly recommending evasive action, with only as much hypocrisy as the case required; and Coleridge was right not to want to praise a God who made vast punishments the sanction for unnatural and useless regulations. One might answer, indeed, that he did worse; he turned the crime into something which hardly any of his readers could accept as a crime, deliberately writing a kind of parody of the traditional struggle for atonement. Just before the *Mariner* he was writing another study of remorse, "The Wanderings of Cain," and the surviving fragments show the same twist in his attitude. Cain out of remorse plans to sacrifice his son, but the ghost of Abel solemnly warns him against it. The initial fault of Cain had been "neglecting to make a proper use of his senses." A spirit advises Cain to blind himself as a means of expiation, but he decides that this would make him morally worse, still further from proper use of his senses. The Spirit turns into a flame and flees down athwart the jagged peaks of the mountain range, so we know its advice was wrong—an insinuating asceticism has been defeated. Evidently, what Coleridge wanted to write about was uncaused guilt, even though the story he was using made the idea particularly hard to convey; no wonder he gave up "Cain" when he found a more suitable story.

VIII

I need to fit "Christabel" and "Kubla Khan" into this account, which may be done fairly briefly. Coleridge soon realised that the *Mariner* was a grander poem than he had expected, and tried to repeat the formula; that is, a large historical period or event was to be illuminated by the reader's intuitive knowledge of the psychology of superstition. To do a Gothic narrative poem was an obvious test; all along, the great buildings of the Middle Ages had been hard for the Augustans to ignore, so the Romantics in trying to escape from the Augustans made immediate use of them. But the sensational Gothic tradition derived largely from anti-Catholic propaganda, too sectarian for Coleridge, and after rejecting that (I think) he just could not see any point in his medieval witch. The end as it stands, the conclusion to Part II, does find a psychological truth in a superstition; it compares witchcraft to an affectionate pretence of cruelty; but this is painfully thin and laboured. It is much to the credit of Coleridge if he refused to finish "Christabel" merely because he found it was a silly superstition, with no philosophical meaning (and Scott just cashed in on the new invention regardless); or he may, as he said, have been inspired by Crashaw's *Hymn to St. Theresa*, and then found the combination of sexuality and desire for martyrdom too nauseating. Though so good in detail, the poem hardly reaches a point where my account can be tested.

"Kubla Khan," however, comes out well. Like House, I find it a completely achieved poem; probably Coleridge was lying when he told the story about the person from Porlock, nearly twenty years later after Byron had succeeded in overcoming his deep shyness about printing it at all. When you realise what it means, you are not surprised that he felt shy. It is a grand though brief statement of the claims of the Romantic artist, and no wonder Coleridge when a failure could not face that. Sir Herbert Read in *The True Voice of Feeling* (1953) gave I think the best account of the Romantic position, which he thinks was first formulated by Schelling but widely acted upon beforehand. A society is always in development, and an artist has a function in it like that of the designer of fashions; the ladies know they want something, but only after seeing the new models can they say "I know what I was wanting; it was that." The paradox of the artist is thus the opposite of the Christian one; he must say ruthlessly what he himself likes or wants, and only by this selfishness can he help his fellows. It is assumed that they all have the same unconscious desires, since they belong to the same developing society and are subject to its pressures; otherwise the self-expression of one could not help the others. The theory had always been true, but the Romantics were the first artists to discover it and act upon it; if they appear ridiculously self-centred, we must remember they considered it a duty. It is in this sense, of course, that the poet is the unacknowledged legislator of the world. By the comparison to the dress designer I do not mean to make the belief ridiculous but to convey how literally it was held, and how rapid the effects were expected to be; also the French Revolution introduced a new pace for the changes of fashion in female dress, and we are still living by it. Every girl must grow up thinking "Poor Mum looked a frump at my age"—there has to be a radical change every generation; before 1789 the process took several generations, and mercifully it has not been getting quicker than the pace then established. Coleridge thus lived in a world which literally did have a heightened sense of changes of fashion. But the original creative genius for which society craved usually emerged from poverty or remote solitude; in music he actually did often come from some unexpected part of Europe, drawing upon its folk songs. He would then be said to "conquer Paris" and so forth; comparing him to Jenghis Khan was practically a cliché, though when expanded into a poem it somehow became "obscure."

After writing a very good poem about the European maritime expansion, it was natural for Coleridge to think of the immediately previous world conquest, of the land mass by Mongols. The story was a familiar one to his mind, and ought to be to ours; it is important for us to understand that the Mongol ponies were cantering up to destroy our society root and branch, in the neighbourhood of Vienna, when another pony galloped up from behind with the news that Mangu Khan had died in Karakorum; so the ponies all turned round and cantered back, to a family share-out of the world conquest; and in the next generation, when they came westwards again, it was known that the rich loot was all in the south, so the Hounds of God destroyed the great civilisation of the Moslems. This caused the Arab inferiority to ourselves which we take for granted; but the reason we were spared was that we were notoriously inferior to them. I thus feel irritated when students placidly call "Kubla" "exotic," meaning, "I won't be bothered with anything outside Europe." Besides, the stories about the Khans are terrible; if you know them, you realise that it is a startling thing to say "That, at bottom, is what an artist is like." The revolution which he brings may do good in the end, but at the time, if it is any good, it will be considered wicked as well as terrible. Coleridge was by no means a hard man, and maybe the grimness of the meaning of the poem, rather than its pathetic contrast with his actual failure, was what made him twenty years later pretend that he had composed it while asleep.

In all three poems an Inside needed to be related to an Outside, a psychology to a history; and I think that only cases like these allow a useful sense to Mr. Eliot's term "objective correlative"—one does not say over the telephone "Do come to dinner on Thursday; and look, I'd be awfully pleased if you could bring your *stomach* with you this time," because it is not expected to be detachable. The phrase was first used about *Hamlet*, and there I do not see the application. But it genuinely is I think a source of the magical power of *The Ancient Mariner* that the inside can be felt to be far from the outside (rather as the children, who have been its greatest admirers, are not really explorers) and yet somehow they keep fitting one another perfectly.

Representation in
The Ancient Mariner

Geoffrey H. Hartman

The Borderers was completed in autumn 1797; less than a year later *Lyrical Ballads* appeared, the fruit of a collaboration between two very different poets. Coleridge's chief contribution, and his most famous poem, bears points of resemblance to *The Borderers* which have not been remarked. *The Ancient Mariner*, according to Coleridge, came out of an abortive attempt of the two poets to compose a joint narrative on "The Wanderings of Cain." Wordsworth's play, completed as *The Ancient Mariner* began to be conceived, has been compared to it only in respect to the crime-punishment-remorse sequence which Coleridge had already labored in *Osorio*. There is, however, a more inclusive connection between the two; like *The Borderers*, but with an unparalleled purity of conception, Coleridge's poem traces the "dim and perilous way" of a soul that has broken with nature and feels the burdenous guilt of selfhood.

The *crime*, first of all, is purified of all extrinsic causes, even of possible motive. It is a founding gesture, or caesura dividing stages of being. It may anticipate the modern "acte gratuite" or reflect the willfulness in Original Sin, but only because both are epochal and determining acts of individuation. The *punishment*, moreover, is simply life itself under the condition of consciousness. Death or self-forgetfulness is not allowed: the Mariner becomes "A man by pain and thought compelled to live." Each man, to become a man, must pass through those straits of individuation, which

From *Wordsworth's Poetry 1787–1814*. © 1964 and 1971 by Yale University. Yale University Press, 1971. Originally entitled "From 'Salisbury Plain' to 'The Ruined Cottage.' " Also from two chapters in *The Fate of Reading*. © 1975 by The University of Chicago. The University of Chicago Press, 1975. Originally entitled "Christopher Smart's *Magnificat*" and "Evening Star and Evening Land."

Coleridge, like Wordsworth, could see as a summation of natural process rather than as an alienation from it:

> In Man the centripetal and individualizing tendency of all Nature is itself concentered and individualized—he is a revelation of Nature! Henceforward, he is referred to himself, delivered up to his own charge; and he who stands the most on himself, and stands the firmest, is the truest, because the most individual, Man. . . . Nor does the form of polarity, which has accompanied the law of individuation up its whole ascent, desert it here. . . . As the ideal genius and the originality, in the same proportion must be the resignation to the real world, the sympathy and the inter-communion with Nature. In the conciliating mid-point or equator, does the Man live, and only by its equal presence in both poles can that life be manifested!

The coincidence of theme is supported by certain details. In *The Ancient Mariner*, as in *The Borderers*, the birth to self-consciousness is linked to the killing of an innocent being. Wordsworth himself suggested the form of the Mariner's crime. "Suppose, said I, you represent him as having killed one of these birds on entering the South Sea, and that the tutelary Spirits of those regions take upon them to avenge the crime." It is Wordsworth, of course, who is haunted by spirit of place, and the "tutelary Spirits" are mythical representations of something he has wished to express in realistic fashion since "The Vale of Esthwaite." The archaic fear that the presence of man violates nature is probably related to the fact that consciousness *appears* as a breach or betrayal of nature.

A second detail, also connected with the imaginative-moral influence of place, is the becalming so vividly described in Coleridge's poem (section 2) and anticipated by Oswald's experience:

The wind fell;

> We lay becalmed week after week, until
> The water of the vessel was exhausted;
> I felt a double fever in my veins,
> Yet rage suppressed itself;—to a deep stillness
> Did my pride tame my pride;—for many days,
> On a dead sea under a burning sky,
> I brooded o'er my injuries, deserted
> By man and nature;—if a breeze had blown,
> It might have found its way into my heart,
> And I had been—no matter—do you mark me?
>
> (IV. 1692–1702)

A link is already made, here, between a stasis in nature and a stasis in the soul. Selfhood manifests its weight, and thought is fixed to a single thought. This constitutes one of the clearest perils of emergent self-consciousness. The beautiful formula, "to a deep stillness / Did my pride tame my pride," intimates not only inner conflict but also how energetically the divided self seeks recomposition. All the energy of the man goes inward; and, as in *The Ancient Mariner*, an external deliverance—"a breeze," an action of grace or nature—is needed before the spell can be broken even in part.

II

Representation implies that the subject cannot be adequately "present" in his own person or substance, so that advocacy is called for. The reason for this "absence," compensated for by "representation," can be various. In legal or ritual matters, the subject may not be of age or not competent. But even when he is competent, of age, fully presentable, situations arise which produce a fiction of his having to be "seconded": in presentation at court (and sometimes in courts of law) he does not appear by himself but needs the support of someone already admitted into the superior presence.

The self does not, of course, disappear into its representative, for then the means would defeat the end, which remains self-presentation. Even in visionary poetry, which so clearly sublimes the self into the other, or exalts the other into quasi-supernatural otherness, the self persists in selfhood. Though Charles Lamb is right in remarking that Coleridge's Ancient Mariner "undergoes such trials as overwhelm and bury all individuality or memory of what he was—like the state of a man in a bad dream, one terrible peculiarity of which is that all consciousness of personality is gone," the spectral happenings in the poem actually doom the Mariner to survival. He is unable to die, or find release from his experience except in the "punctual agony" of storytelling.

Whether or not this doom of deathlessness is preferable to nothingness—"Who would lose," says Milton's Belial, "Though full of pain, this intellectual being, / Those thoughts that wander through Eternity, / To perish rather, swallow'd up and lost / In the wide womb of uncreated night . . ."—the self can never be so sublimated, or so objectified, that only its representative is left. Even granted that self desires an absolute escape from self, what would be satisfied by that escape: indeed would anything of self be left to register the satisfaction? To urge questions of this kind is to approach psychoanalysis, but at the same time to link it with speculations on the sublime going back at least to Edmund Burke. These speculations ponder the vertiginous relation between self-loss and self-aggrandizement.

Let me return briefly to Coleridge's poem. Why does the Mariner kill the albatross? A fascinating question; but even the simplest answer, that it was willfulness, implies a drive on the Mariner's part for self-presence. The killing is a shadow of the Mariner's own casting. What follows his self-determining, self-inaugural act is, paradoxically, the presence of otherness. In seeking to "emerge," the self experiences separation anxieties, and these express themselves in motions akin to the defense mechanism of "beautiful indifference" (noted by Charcot in patients suffering from hysteria) as well as to the terror which may accompany isolation.

At the same time, there is a movement toward atonement (at-one-ment, reconciliation) in Coleridge's poem. "Representation" cannot be divorced from advocacy. You justify either the self or that which stands greatly against it: perhaps both at once. The situation could be likened to a trial, though not to one resulting in a definite verdict. The trouble with this line of inquiry is that too many metaphors come into play until one begins to move within art's own richness of thematic variation. Yet such metaphors as trial, court, theater, debut and so on, converge on the idea of a place of heightened demand and intensified consciousness. "The daemon," says Yeats, ". . . brings man again and again to the place of choice, heightening temptation that the choice may be as final as possible . . ." Let us consider the nature of this "place," imagined or real.

III

So the Valley of Chamouny [in "Hymn before Sun-rise, in the Vale of Chamouni"] is truly a "Valley of Wonders." But does the poet succeed in "reconquering" his "substance" there? It is hard to say, from the Hymn, whether loss of self or loss of voice was more important. Yet writing the Hymn meant recovering a voice. In the Hymn as in the Rime, release from the curse—that dread stillness, or paralysis of motion—is obtained by the ability to pray. And prayer is interpreted in both poems as praise:

> O happy living things! no tongue
> Their beauty might declare

The weight of the Albatross (like the air's "ebon mass") is removed, together with the stone from the tongue.

Yet voice remains uneasy, both in the Hymn and in the Rime. Praise mutes itself in the act:

> O happy living things! no tongue
> Their beauty might declare:
> A spring of love gushed from my heart
> And I blessed them unaware

There is too great a contrast between the compulsive speech of the Mariner and this first, tongueless moment. The Hymn, similarly, is hardly an "unaware" blessing: its one moment of sweet unconsciousness (ll. 17–23) does not compensate us for the forced sublimity of the rest.

Praise, according to the Psalmist, is a "sacrifice of thanksgiving." It substitutes for, or sublimates, the rite of blood sacrifice. The Hymn on Mont Blanc is written against this background of sublimation. The exact pressure put on Coleridge—the offering demanded of him by the dread form—we shall never know. Coleridge's "Sca'fell Letter" shows him as "overawed," but there was nothing necessarily mysterious. He felt, that much is certain, a loss of substance, a passivity both shaming and sublime—and he recovers himself, at least in the Hymn, by the will of his voice; more precisely, by the willed imitation of a sublime voice.

I will not deny that the inferred human situation is more impressive than the Hymn produced by it. But that is because, in Coleridge, poetry remains so closely linked to sublimation. Sublimation always sacrifices to an origin stronger than itself. If it did not cherish or dread this origin—this "hiding-place" of power—it would not shroud it from sight by displacement or falsification:

> Never mortal saw
> The cradle of the strong one,
> Never mortal heard
> The gathering of his voices;
> The deep-murmured charm

Such "wildly-silent" scenes are not infrequent in Coleridge. He is often, in fancy, near an origin where a "great Spirit" with "plastic sweep"—the wind or voice of the opening of Genesis—moves on the still darkness. But he is, at the same time, so removed from this primal scene that it becomes a "stilly murmur" which "tells of silence." The voice redeeming that silence, or vexed into being by it, can be as cold as the eye of Ancient Mariner or moon.

The Rime of the Ancient Mariner as Epic Symbol

Warren Stevenson

In *Anatomy of Criticism*, Northrop Frye refers to the "miniature epic" as the development which occurs "when a lyric on a conventional theme achieves a concentration that expands it into a miniature epic: if not the historical 'little epic' or epyllion, something very like it generically." Frye cites "Lycidas" and Spenser's "Epithalamion," as well as "the later poems of Eliot, of Edith Sitwell, and many cantos of Pound," as examples of the genre. I would like to suggest that Coleridge's *Rime of the Ancient Mariner* may profitably be seen as a miniature epic. It is of medium length, and sets out to teach a people something of their own traditions. It employs the supernatural. Also, the action involves a voyage around the world which begins and ends in the same place, more or less as the total action of the *Odyssey* extends from Ithaca to Troy and back to Ithaca, and likewise involves strange sea adventures.

Frye also employs the term "epos" to describe works in which the radical of presentation is oral address, and says it "takes in all literature in verse or prose, which makes some attempt to preserve the convention of recitation and a listening audience." *The Rime of the Ancient Mariner*, with its narrating Mariner and Wedding-Guest who "cannot choose but hear," makes an attempt to preserve such a convention, albeit contained within a larger narrative framework. The usual generic designation for the poem is "literary ballad," which means that we know who the poet is, but he is

From *Dalhousie Review* 56, no. 3 (Autumn 1976). © 1976 by Dalhousie University Press.

trying to be primitive. *The Ancient Mariner* is thus both literary ballad and miniature epic, narrative and displaced epos.

Like "Kubla Khan" and "Christabel," *The Ancient Mariner* has at least part of its setting in the later Middle Ages. The instrument with which the Mariner kills the Albatross, the arbalest or crossbow, was used chiefly during the twelfth and thirteenth centuries, and gave way to the longbow in the fourteenth century. The poem's Christian context is carefully established by means of the reference to "kirk" in line 23, and by other details, such as "Christian soul," "vespers nine," and "Heaven's Mother," mentioned subsequently in the narrative. So the background of the Mariner's narrative is both medieval and Christian.

William Empson suggests that the poem is "about the European maritime expansion," and, in passing, that "The effect on literature of [Europeans'] maritime empires was to make the explorer a symbol of scientific discovery . . . thence of intellectual adventure in general, and at last for the highest event in ethics, the moral discovery, which gets a man called a traitor by his own society." Since the Mariner's two-hundred shipmates represent his own society, and that society was medieval and Christian, it follows that the Mariner as intellectual and moral rebel against that society represents the Renaissance with its new learning, particularly its new science, which was anathema to the old order. Seen in this light, the poem recapitulates a major aspect of European history from the medieval to the modern period.

For the Mariner is not simply an explorer; he is discoverer of the Pacific and, if we are to trust the poem's inner dynamics, the world's first circumnavigator. True, we are not told specifically which way the Mariner's ship returned from the Pacific to his own country; nor, for that matter, are we told which way the Mariner's ship got into the Pacific. Bernard Smith, in an article entitled "Coleridge's *Ancient Mariner* and Cook's Second Voyage," argues that the course of the Mariner's journey closely corresponds to that of the *Resolution*, Cook's ship, which circumnavigated the world by proceeding via the southern ice fields in an eastward direction:

> Critics of the *Ancient Mariner* tend to assume that Coleridge intended it to be understood that the Mariner's vessel doubled Cape Horn, the two lines, "the Sun came up upon the left" and "the Sun now rose upon the right" being cited in support. A moment's reflection, however, will make one realize that as soon as the vessel began to move northwards instead of southwards the sun would rise upon the right. . . . Immediately following the lines

> The ice did split with a thunder-fit;
> The helmsman steered us through!

we have the line

> And a good south wind sprung up behind.

Such a wind in the region of the prevailing westerlies would drive a ship eastwards. When this is read in conjunction with the accompanying gloss which tells how the Albatross followed the ship "as it returned northwards through fog and floating ice" a more feasible interpretation than the doubling of the Horn is that the vessel is moving into the southern Indian Ocean.

Smith's argument may seem attractive, particularly if one assumes, as he does, that Coleridge was likely to have had a single source in mind for the Mariner's voyage. Against this theory of an eastward circumnavigation, however, is most readers' spontaneous response to the lines

> We were the first that ever burst
> Into that silent sea.
>
> (105–6)

Lowes observes that these lines echo Sir John Narborough's account of Magellan's entry into the Pacific. George Shelvocke's *Voyage round the World by the way of the Great South Sea*, whose influence on the poem was first noticed by Wordsworth, also describes a westward circumnavigation. And as for the south wind, there is the frequency of south winds in the neighbourhood of the Antarctic Circle reported by all explorers.

The hypothesis of a westward direction for the Mariner's journey also receives poetic support. For the Romantics, the West was the region of new life and new hope, fraught with infinite possibilities for cosmic renewal or cosmic betrayal. The motif of the westward journey becomes something of an archetype in Romantic poetry, extending as it does from Blake's

> To find the Western path
> Right thro' the Gates of Wrath

through Wordsworth's "Stepping Westward" to the westward-looking conclusion of Keats's "To My Brother George," to mention but three of the possible examples. And the Ancient Mariner is "looking westward" when he beholds the spectre bark, which seems to be coming from unknown and as-yet-unexplored regions.

Moreover, the sense of physical and intellectual daring which permeates the poem and for which spirits as well as mariners are famous seems to

require a westward journey and a return route from the Pacific to the
Atlantic via the Cape of Good Hope. The gloss which Coleridge added to
the 1817 version of the poem helps to make this clear. The Line, or equator,
is mentioned three times, once each in parts 1, 2, and 5, as it would have
to be crossed at least twice in a circumnavigational voyage, and was evidently touched once in the Pacific, where the ship was becalmed (ll. 105–14).
This is not, as has been suggested, a mistake on Coleridge's part. Each
mention of the Line is accompanied by a description of the vertical sun
standing over the mast at noon (ll. 30, 112–13, 383). The absence of any
further reference to extreme cold after Part 1 indicates that the lonesome
spirit from the South Pole carries the ship from the equatorial calm in the
Pacific southward around Southeast Asia and the Cape of Good Hope, and
then northward as far as the Line in the Atlantic, where his jurisdiction
ends and the ship is propelled "northward" by angelic power for the re-
mainder of the journey. It is surely more than a mere coincidence that the
Polar Spirit's jurisdiction over the Mariner and his vessel ends at the precise
point where he has completed his circumnavigation. The poem's structure
as miniature epic also seems to require that the Mariner's journey should
represent a completed cycle.

The Mariner as the world's first circumnavigator anticipates Magellan.
He also anticipates, as has recently been observed, all those subsequent
voyages of exploration and discovery by means of which Western European
society has sought to imprint its imperial and slave-owning image upon
the New World. But the specific milieu of the Mariner's narration is late
medieval, and he commits a specific crime which places him in violation
of that society's code. In the final versions of the poem, at least, it does not
appear that the Albatross was slain for food; nor is there any reference to
its having been eaten. (Empson, relying on such details as the reference to
"biscuit-worms" in earlier versions of the poem, argues that the Albatross
was shot for food and eaten. His argument, though plausible, receives no
confirmation from the final text, however.) Rather, Coleridge emphasizes
the apparent motivelessness of the Mariner's act to make it appear as an act
of will standing in violation of both social mores (the sailors' taboo, which
Coleridge may have invented) and extrinsic reason. The Mariner's sin
against the Holy Ghost, or Spirit of Love, is parallel to the displacement
of Love by logic as the raison d'être of the cosmos, a displacement which
began during the Renaissance with the discoveries not only of Columbus
and Magellan but also those of Galileo and Kepler.

The instrument with which the Mariner commits his crime, the crossbow, serves a dual function in that it helps to place the Mariner's narration

within its medieval context and also, as an instrument of mechanical precision, anticipates those technological changes which revolutionized European society during the following centuries. No doubt it also bears an
ironic relation to the cross of Christianity. The spirit of mankind, or so it
seemed to the Romantics, was becoming crucified upon a cross of tech-
nology. Another instrument of precision referred to in the poem's imagery
is the plumb line: after the Mariner spontaneously blesses the water snakes,
"The Albatross fell off, and sank / Like lead into the sea" (209–91). And
after the circumnavigational voyage is completed, "The ship went down
like lead" (549). The mysterious motion of the ship, while intended to be
supernatural in origin, also has technological overtones. Specifically, the
motion without wind described in part 6 of the poem suggests not so much
nautical, as aeronautical motion:

First Voice

"But why drives on that ship so fast,
Without or wave or wind?"

Second Voice

"The air is cut away before
And closes from behind."

(422–25)

As the gloss puts it, "the angelic power causeth the vessel to drive northward
faster than human life could endure." The Mariner's voyage is thus not
only a voyage through space but a voyage through time as well. For better
or worse, he emerges as the first modern man.

Indeed, there are strong hints that the transition from the Middle Ages
to the Renaissance has already been effected between the time when the
Mariner made his voyage and the time when he narrates it to the Wedding-
Guest:

We were the first that ever burst
Into that silent sea.

(105–6)

The statement that the Mariner and his companions were the first suggests
that others have since duplicated the feat. The Mariner's story, as we have
seen, is pre-Magellan and medieval in setting; its narration to the Wedding-
Guest is post-Magellan. The bassoon, the sound of which interrupts the
Mariner's narration (1. 32), was invented in the sixteenth century. Thus,

an interval of at least two hundred years has elapsed between the time when the Mariner set out on his voyage and the time when he narrates it to the Wedding-Guest. This is a consideration the importance of which has not been sufficiently appreciated. It means that the poem embodies in its very structure that transition from the medieval to the modern world which also constitutes a major aspect of its theme.

The Mariner's attempt to return to the old dispensation, symbolized by the kirk and by the Mariner's concluding advice to the Wedding-Guest, is only partially successful. It is an attempt which finds its parallel in the cry of "Back to the Middle Ages" which reverberates through the nineteenth century and on into the twentieth century, particularly among members of the younger generation. But the Mariner's circumnavigation of the earth may also be seen as a symbol of those changes which have taken place since the Renaissance, both in a geopolitical and a technological sense, so that the repentant Mariner may after all be seen as the first lonely inhabitant of the global village.

Coleridge and the Deluded Reader:
The Rime of the Ancient Mariner

Frances Ferguson

The criticism of *The Rime of the Ancient Mariner* reflects a craving for causes. Opium, or Coleridge's guilt-obsessed personality, or (as Robert Penn Warren would have it) his convergent beliefs in the "One Life within us all" and in the Imagination caused the poem to come into being in its own peculiar form. A "teaching text" like *The Norton Anthology of English Literature* sets out to explicate the lines (all direct quotations from the *Rime* follow the text of *The Complete Poetical Works of Samuel Taylor Coleridge*, ed. Ernest Hartley Coleridge, Oxford, 1968):

> The Wedding-Guest stood still,
> And listens like a three years' child:
> The Mariner hath his will
>
> (ll. 14–16)

—and sets up a nice causal connection by asserting that "the Mariner has gained control of the will of the Wedding-Guest by hypnosis—or, as it was called in Coleridge's time—by 'mesmerism.'" There may be some form of hypnosis—or mesmerism—in the rather monotonous rhythms of the lines, but the annotation converts hypnosis into a misguidedly "scientific" explanation of why the Wedding-Guest couldn't or didn't bother to get away.

This construction of causes—for the poem as a whole or for individual passages—is particularly striking because it appears as a series of belated

From *Georgia Review* 31, no. 3 (Fall 1977). © 1977 by The University of Georgia.

rejoinders to the many complaints that greeted the poem's first public appearance. The *Rime* was quite widely censured for extravagance, unconnectedness, and improbability. Even Wordsworth in his Note to the *Rime* in the 1800 edition of *Lyrical Ballads* registered various objections that amounted to the assertion that the poem was deficient in connections and causes:

> The Poem of my Friend has indeed great defects; first, that the principal person has no distinct character, either in his profession of Mariner, or as a human being who having been long under the control of supernatural impressions might be supposed himself to partake of something supernatural: secondly, that he does not act, but is continually acted upon: thirdly, that the events having no necessary connection do not produce each other; and lastly, that the imagery is somewhat too laboriously accumulated.

Wordsworth's account of the poem's "defects" in a note that is a manifesto for its being reprinted may well be of a piece with the simultaneously published Preface to *Lyrical Ballads*, in which he sought to avoid the appearance of *"reasoning* [the reader] into an approbation of these particular Poems." Everywhere in his account of defects Wordsworth cites formal features (albeit in the extended sense)—character, plot, motive, and imagery; and it is hard to believe that Wordsworth was doing anything more than repeating—and thereby acknowledging—the categories of poetic appreciation that he and Coleridge were explicitly attacking in *Lyrical Ballads*. But if the author of "The Thorn," "We are seven," and *The Prelude* seems improbable in the role of someone wedded to clearly delineated character, plot, motive, and imagery, Coleridge's own remarks about the poem are even more difficult to assimilate to the critical search for causes and consequences. For example, Coleridge's famous account of Mrs. Barbauld's opinion of the *Rime* figures in almost every article on the poem, but to diverse ends:

> MRS. BARBAULD once told me that she admired the Ancient Mariner very much, but that there were two faults in it,—it was improbable, and had no moral. As for the probability, I owned that that might admit some question; but as to the want of a moral, I told her that in my own judgment the poem had too much; and that the only or chief fault, if I might say so, was the obtrusion of the moral sentiment so openly on the reader as a

principle or cause of action in a work of such pure imagination. It ought to have had no more moral than the Arabian Nights' tale of the merchant's sitting down to eat dates by the side of a well, and throwing the shells aside, and lo! a geni starts up, and says he *must* kill the aforesaid merchant, *because* one of the date-shells had, it seems, put out the eye of the geni's son.

(*Specimens of the Table Talk of the late Samuel Taylor Coleridge*)

On the one hand, critics have harnessed this passage to an attempt to eschew interpretation; the poem as a "work of . . . pure imagination" has no discursively translatable meaning. (This is the "What-do-you-think-when-you-think-nothing?" school of criticism.) On the other hand, perhaps the most influential modern critic of the poem, Warren, confesses that he is "inclined to sympathize with the lady's desire that poetry have some significant relation to the world, some meaning." Thus, his reading of the passage from *Table Talk* about Mrs. Barbauld is this: "If the passage affirms anything, it affirms that Coleridge intended the poem to have a 'moral sentiment,' but felt that he had been a trifle unsubtle in fulfilling his intention."

The no-moral position seems patenty unconvincing because it becomes an excuse for hanging in one's confusions; but even though Warren's essay remains the most provocative interpretation, it also seems progressively to overspecify the "moral sentiment." What Warren calls the sacramental vision, the theme of the "One Life" that is expressed in the poem's conclusion ("He prayeth best") and what he calls the imagination (the symbols of the poem) are both models of unity and fusion. And since unity and coherence are poetry for Warren, this poem must be both unified and unifying by definition; images must be symbols, and the symbols must speak of the Mariner's—and the reader's—"expressive integration" with the universe and "with other men, with society." Warren's interpretation suggests not merely that the sin of pride is involved in the *Rime* but also that the poem in some sense involves teaching one—all of us—to avoid that sin. But while I agree with Warren that morals are at issue in the poem, Coleridgean morality seems to me consistently more problematic than he suggests. For the difficulty of the poem is that the possibility of learning from the Mariner's experience depends upon sorting that experience into a more linear and complete pattern than the poem ever agrees to do. For the poem seems almost as thorough a work of backwardness—or hysteron proteron—as we have.

One aspect of this backwardness led a contemporary reviewer (Charles

Burney) to fulminate in 1799 against *Lyrical Ballads* in general and against the *Rime* in particular:

> Though we have been extremely entertained with the fancy, the facility, and (in general) the sentiments, of these pieces, we cannot regard them as *poetry*, of a class to be cultivated at the expence of a higher species of versification, unknown in our language at the time when our elder writers, whom this author condescends to imitate, wrote their ballads. Would it not be degrading poetry, as well as the English language, to go back to the barbarous and uncouth numbers of Chaucer? . . . Should we be gainers by the retrogradations? . . . None but savages have submitted to eat acorns after corn was found.
>
> (Coleridge: The Critical Heritage, ed. J. R. deJ. Jackson)

But the archaistic diction is only one aspect of the poem's "retrogradation." For Coleridge not only reverses linguistic and poetic *progress* in the *Rime*, he so thoroughly compounds the past with the present tense that the action or progress of the poem hovers in a temporal limbo:

> The Wedding-Guest he beat his breast,
> Yet he cannot choose but hear;
> And thus spake on that ancient man,
> The bright-eyed Mariner.
>
> (ll. 37–40)

And even such a basic question as that of the Mariner's motive for killing the bird is given a tardy (and insufficient) answer. The event of the killing is recounted in the first section of the poem; and the suggestion that the Mariner may have been trying to confute his shipmates' superstitious connections between the Albatross and the weather emerges only in the second section. The possibility that the Mariner may have hoped—scientifically—to disprove their superstition is the closest thing to a hypothesis we are offered, and it appears only when we desire a motive so strongly that we must mistrust our own efforts to reestablish a cause-and-effect sequence.

But how does any reader, any critic sort out the action that presumably points the moral of the poem? Or, in other words, how does one sort out the moral value of the agents of the poem? The Mariner concludes his story to the Wedding-Guest with the following "good" words:

> He prayeth well, who loveth well
> Both man and bird and beast.

> He prayeth best, who loveth best
> All things both great and small;
> For the dear God who loveth us,
> He made and loveth all.
>
> (ll. 612–17)

But the Mariner has a decidedly malignant effect on the persons who save his body after his spiritual redemption on the ship: the Pilot collapses in a fit, and the Pilot's boy goes mad. Likewise, the Albatross seems good, then bad, then good, because the death of the Albatross causes first fog and mist (bad), then clearing (good), and finally the failure of the breeze (bad). Our difficulty is that all the evidences of moral value are mutually contradictory.

There is, however, one element of the poem that leads us. In 1815–16 Coleridge added the Gloss along the left margin as he was readying his work for the 1817 edition of *Sibylline Leaves*. And the critical "advances" that have been made in the last century and a half pay tribute to Coleridge's sagacity in having supplied this helpful commentary. John Livingston Lowes notes the literary elegance of the Gloss's prose. B. R. McElderry, Jr., sees the Gloss as an "artistic restatement and ornament of what is obvious in the text," and as a chance for Coleridge to relive the pleasure of writing his "one completed masterpiece." And Robert Penn Warren peppers his long essay on the *Rime* with statements like this: "The Gloss here tells us all we need to know, defining the Mariner's relation to the moon." The almost universal opinion seems to be that Coleridge wrote the Gloss (either as Coleridge or in the role of a fictitious editor) because he was attempting to clarify and unify the poem after entertaining the legion of hostile comments upon its confusions and inconsequence.

But the Gloss provides a strange kind of clarity and unity. Consider some examples. As the Wedding-Guest speaks for the first time about anything except the wedding he wishes he could attend, this is what the text offers:

> "God save thee, ancient Mariner!
> From the fiends, that plague thee thus!—
> Why look'st thou so?"—With my cross-bow
> I shot the ALBATROSS.
>
> (ll. 79–82)

And the Gloss comments—"The ancient Mariner inhospitably killeth the pious bird of good omen." "Inhospitably," "pious," and "good omen" bespeak conclusions that do not echo the main text because the main text never reaches such value judgments.

The Argument that Coleridge deleted from the poem after 1800 recounted that "the Ancient Mariner cruelly and in contempts of the laws of hospitality killed a Sea-bird," but the Gloss here seems even stronger than the Argument had been. However forceful the ancient laws of hospitality, the notion of a man's hospitality toward a bird contains a rather anomalous and itself prideful assumption—that the bird is a visitor in the Mariner's domain. If the Mariner commits a sin of pride in killing the Albatross and thereby asserting his power over it, even the Mariner's refusal to kill the bird would in this context involve the pride-laden assurance that man's domain measures the universe. But the even more striking feature of the Gloss is the attribution of unambiguous moral qualities to the bird—"the pious bird of good omen." And while the text of the poem proper registers only the sailors' vacillations on the moral standing of the bird, the Gloss is conspicuously conclusive on that point. The main text offers the sailors' contradictory opinions:

> And I had done a hellish thing,
> And it would work 'em woe:
> For all averred, I had killed the bird
> That made the breeze to blow.
> Ah wretch! said they, the bird to slay,
> That made the breeze to blow!
>
> Nor dim nor red, like God's own head,
> The glorious Sun uprist:
> Then all averred, I had killed the bird
> That brought the fog and mist.
> 'Twas right, said they, such birds to slay,
> That brought the fog and mist.
>
> (ll. 91–102)

And the Gloss seems merely to scorn the sailors' confusions: first "His shipmates cry out against the ancient Mariner, for killing the bird of good luck"; then, "But when the fog cleared off, they justify the same, and thus make themselves accomplices in the crime."

When the ship is stalled, and everyone aboard is desperately searching the horizon in hope of rescue, the text recounts things this way:

> A weary time! a weary time!
> How glazed each weary eye,
> When looking westward, I beheld
> A something in the sky.

> At first it seemed a little speck,
> And then it seemed a mist;
> It moved and moved, and took at last
> A certain shape, I wist.
>
> (ll. 145–52)

And the Gloss makes this remark: "The Ancient Mariner beholdeth a sign in the element afar off." Nothing is ever really "afar off" for the Gloss. What for the main text is merely "a something" and "a certain shape" is already categorized for the Gloss as a sign, a symbol. The Gloss, in assuming that things must be significant and interpretable, finds significance and interpretability, but only by reading ahead of—or beyond—the main text.

Now the only portion of the Gloss that has been cited as an editorializing incursion upon the main text is the scholarly comment that supports the dreams which some of the sailors have about an avenging spirit: "A Spirit had followed them; one of the invisible inhabitants of this planet, neither departed souls nor angels; concerning whom the learned Jew, Josephus, and the Platonic Constantinopolitan, Michael Psellus, may be consulted. They are very numerous, and there is no climate or element without one or more." But both the entire Gloss and the bulk of critical opinion of the poem may well be editorializing, in that they mold contradictory evidences into a cause-and-effect pattern that the main text never quite offers: the Albatross was a good bird, the Mariner killed it, the Mariner was punished for his crime, the Mariner learned to acknowledge the beauty of all natural creatures and was saved to proselytize for this eminently noble moral position.

But let us return to the remarks on the poem in the *Specimens of the Table Talk of the late Samuel Taylor Coleridge*; in Coleridge's account of the first tale from the *Arabian Nights* the geni "says he *must* kill the aforesaid merchant, *because* one of the date-shells had, it seems, put out the eye of the geni's son" (emphasis Coleridge's). If the poem should have had no more moral than this, we may ask, what kind of moral is it? The merchant, presumably, would not have thrown his date shells into the well if he had dreamed that he would do harm to the geni's son; and by the same logic, the Mariner would, presumably, not have killed the Albatross if he had recognized its goodness and significance. As is common in Coleridge's work generally, intention and effect are absolutely dicontinuous, and the moral is that morality appears to involve certainty only if you can already know the full outcome of every action before you commit it.

Coleridge's recounting his conversation with Mrs. Barbauld about the poem seems to me particularly striking in the context of this moral problem. A rather sizable collection of reviewers had complained about the poem's improbability and lack of moral, but Mrs. Barbauld became his most significant interlocutor on the poem's moral import. A brief excursus on Anna Laetitia Barbauld may suggest why she in particular would be an appropriate real or fictitious disputant of record. Mrs. Barbauld was firmly committed to the education of children, and she demonstrated her commitment by authoring *Lessons for Children* (1780) and *Hymns in Prose for Children* (1781). *Lessons for Children* was divided into four parts—*Lessons . . .* 1) For Children from Two to Three Years Old; 2) and 3) For Children of Three Years Old; and 4) For Children from Three to Four Years Old, so that the readings moved from simple to more complex in a gradual scale. As Mrs. Barbauld stated in her Preface to *Hymns in Prose*, this was her purpose:

> to impress devotional feelings as early as possible on the infant mind . . . to impress them by connecting religion with a variety of sensible objects; with all that he sees, all that he hears, all that affects his young mind with wonder or delight; and thus by deep, strong, and permanent associations to lay the best foundation for practical devotion in future life.

Reading was thus not merely a neutral exercise; reading and religion were to be taught simultaneously. Now in this respect Mrs. Barbauld's project was not exactly unheard of. Such a linkage was explicit in the practice of using the Bible as the textbook for reading; and from the sixteenth century, when people began to be concerned about the heretical interpretations of the Bible that neophyte readers produced, the primer had been seen as a temporary substitute for the Bible or as a preparation for the Bible itself. Additionally the primer was supposed to supply relevance; it would not merely link reading with religion, it would also prepare the child to recognize the moral dilemmas of his everyday life.

Thus, the child learning to read in the late eighteenth and early nineteenth centuries was given (by Mrs. Barbauld, Mrs. Trimmer, Thomas Day, Maria Edgeworth, and others) texts that endowed nature with particular significance for the child, and as a religious child, he was to behave with particular moral probity towards nature. In fact, the most frequently recurrent theme in primer literature of the time was the sinfulness of cruelty to animals—particularly birds. Mrs. Barbauld's *Lessons for Children of Three Years Old*, part 1, in fact, concludes with two short stories, the first of which enforces the moral of kindness to birds:

A naughty boy will not feed a starving and freezing robin; in fact he even pulls the poor bird's tail! It dies. Shortly after that, the boy's parents leave him because he is cruel, and he is forced to beg for food. He goes into a forest, sits down and cries, and is never heard of again; it is believed that bears ate him.

> (SYLVIA W. PATTERSON, *Rousseau's* Emile *And Early Children's Literature*)

No wonder Wordsworth recounts in book 1 of *The Prelude* (ll. 333–50) that his childish act of stealing eggs from a bird's nest produced a major crisis of guilt.

Now I obviously don't mean to suggest either that Coleridge wrote *The Rime of the Ancient Mariner* or that Wordsworth wrote that passage from *The Prelude* as a direct attack on Mrs. Barbauld or primers generally. But I do want to suggest that the moral causality that most critics discern in the *Rime* sounds less appropriate to Coleridge's poem than to the conclusion of Mrs. Barbauld's "Epitaph on a Goldfinch":

> Reader,
> if suffering innocence can hope for retribution,
>   deny not to the gentle shade
>   of this unfortunate captive
>   the natural though uncertain hope
>   of animating some happier form,
>   or trying his new-fledged pinions
>   in some humble Elysium,
>   beyond the reach of Man,
>   the tyrant
>   of this lower universe.
>
> (*Works*, vol. 2)

The primary difference between Mrs. Barbauld's literary morals and Coleridge's seems to lie in her emphasis upon acts and his agonizing explorations of the difficulties of recognizing the full implications of an action before it is committed, put in the context of the full range of human history (particularly the context of the Bible), and interpreted. Mrs. Barbauld's story of the little boy who was cruel to the starving and freezing robin is, one might assert, no less improbable than the *Rime*, no less committed to what we might see as excessive punishment for the crime perpetrated. But while the critics of the *Rime* almost invariably mock Mrs. Barbauld as an obtuse and simplistic moralist, they also subscribe to the moral line of the Gloss, which leads them to a Barbauldian moral.

We must return to a rather simple-minded question: How bad was the Mariner to kill the bird? The act was certainly one of "motiveless malignity," for the Albatross had done nothing to him. But the crucial point is that he "didn't know any better"; it's merely the kind of explanation that enlightened parents of our own century employ to exonerate a child who has just destroyed the drapes in order to "play dress-up" or who has pulled the cat's tail. And while Mrs. Barbauld could be said to regard the learning of reading and morals as *technical* skills, Coleridge recognizes reading as moral because one's *techné* can never suffice. One acts, Coleridge would say, on the basis of one's reading or interpretation, but if reading and interpretation are the genesis of moral action, they may be infinitely divorced for moral outcome—may, in fact, reverse one's interpretation of the moral value of the act. Reading as a *techné* and morals as techniques of behavior thus become suspect for Coleridge because they imply that experience—and one's interpretation of it—are both stable and repetitive—that one can learn what one needs to know.

In this context, Coleridge's Gloss to the *Rime* recalls not merely the archetypal glosses—those in the margins of early printed editions of the Bible; it also raises the question of the ways in which such glosses and the primer tradition made the Bible more accessible and comprehensible while also domesticating that main text. For if glosses and primers came to be felt necessary because readers "couldn't understand" the Bible properly, Coleridge's addition of his Gloss to the *Rime* seems to have answered the critics who called his poem incomprehensible, largely by a domestication. Think back to the main text of the poem. The Wedding-Guest, in the first stanza, asks, "Now wherefore stopp'st thou me?" Nowhere in the poem is the Wedding-Guest's question answered, not even at the end, although we know then:

> He went like one that hath been stunned,
> And is of sense forlorn:
> A sadder and a wiser man,
> He rose the morrow morn.
>
> (ll. 622–25)

The Mariner's stopping the Wedding-Guest is probably the most arbitrary event in a poem filled with arbitrary events, and any explanation that asserts that he was chosen because his callowness needed correction seems far-fetched. The main interest of the Wedding-Guest is that he has something to do. He has the intention of going to a wedding; in part 1 of the poem he alternately pays attention to the Mariner and to the sounds of the wedding; but then, at the end of the poem he turns "from the bridegroom's door." Most importantly, neither his personality nor his intentions matter; he becomes what he reads (or hears). But if this account seems a fabulous escalation of the power of the word, think of the fate of the other sailors on the Mariner's ship. Nothing happens to them when they denounce the Mariner's act of murder, but then they reverse themselves when the fog clears and the fair breeze continues. The Gloss informs us that they thus become accomplices in the Mariner's crime. But in part 3 of the poem, the Mariner is awarded to life-in-death while all the rest of the crew become the property of death. We never know whether this eventuality is a delayed punishment for their first opinion or a more immediate punishment for their second. Since the Mariner did the killing when they only expressed opinions about it, their fate seems cruel indeed. But the implication seems to be that every interpretation involves a moral commitment with consequences that are inevitably more far-reaching and unpredictable than one could have imagined. And neither the sailors' paucity of information (which necessarily produces a limited perspective) nor their intentions (to praise the good and denounce the bad) are any exoneration for them (because most human interpretations are similarly limited, well-intentioned, and unexonerated).

Some of the major revisions of the poem, at least in retrospect, seem designed to make not the moral but the process of arriving at morals the major issue. In 1798 the poem was published under the title, *The Rime of the Ancient Mariner*, and its Argument preceding the text provided rather neutral information, primarily geographical—"How a Ship having passed the Line was driven by storms to the Cold Country towards the South Pole; . . . and of the strange things that befell. . . ." But in keeping with Coleridge's rather persistent practice of giving with one hand while taking away with the other, the 1800 version was titled *The Ancient Mariner: A Poet's Reverie*, as if to emphasize the unreality of the piece, while the Argument was far more morally directive—"how the Ancient Mariner cruelly and in contempt of the laws of hospitality killed a Sea-bird and how he was followed by many and strange Judgements." And a similar doubleness or confusion arises with the introduction of the Gloss in 1817. For while the Gloss sorts out a moral line for the poem, it is accompanied by an epigraph that Coleridge excerpted from Thomas Burnet:

> I believe easily that there are more invisible than visible beings
> in the universe. But of them all, who will tell us the race? and
> the ranks and relationships and differences and functions of each

one? What do they do? What places do they inhabit? The human mind has always circled about the knowledge of these things but has never reached it. Still, it is undeniably desirable to contemplate in the mind, as it were in a picture, the image of a greater and better world: lest the mind, accustomed to the small details of daily life, become contracted and sink entirely into trivial thoughts. But meanwhile we must be watchful of truth and must keep within suitable limits, in order that we may distinguish the certain from the uncertain, day from night.

(Translation of Burnet in Coleridge, *Selected Poetry and Prose*, ed. Elisabeth Schneider)

Although a number of critics have taken the epigraph as an ironic foil to the progress of the poem, its waverings between belief and self-cautionary gestures are closer to the pattern of the main text than has been acknowledged. For here an assertion of belief dissolves into a discourse on the lack of information, while an assertion of the necessity of belief even from limited information dwindles into the necessity of accepting limitation. But the most interesting feature of the epigraph is not primarily what it says but what it refuses to say. For the main text of the *Rime* is written in imitation of medieval ballads; and while the persona of the Gloss is that of a seventeenth-century editor who lays claim to sorting out the medieval tale, the author of the epigraph, his contemporary, merely provides us with a record of his lack of certainty. Thus, for the *Rime*, a mini-epic of progress that moves largely by retrogradation, we have a Gloss of progress and an epigraph that sees the progress of knowledge only in terms of circling— or, perhaps, hanging on the line. Even Coleridge's revisions not only maintain but also intensify the contradictory interpretations that the main text keeps throwing up to us.

As Coleridge would (and did) say, "I would be understood." Although I have criticized (and perhaps even derided) the Gloss and Gloss-bound criticism, I do not mean to suggest simply that the position of the Gloss is wrong and that uncertainty (or no position) is right. That would be to plunge the poem back into the criticism that maintains that the poem doesn't mean anything because it is a "poem . . . of pure imagination." Coleridge vented his spleen against common schemes of the progress of knowledge— the "general conceit that states and governments might be and ought to be constructed as machines, every movement of which might be foreseen and taken into previous calculation" (*Lay Sermons*) and against education infected by "the vile sophistications and mutilations of ignorant mountebanks" (*The*

Friend, Essay 14). But he was equally virulent on the subject of indolence (especially his own) as an attempt to avoid commitment. Commitment— or belief—is inevitable for Coleridge, but it does not issue in certainty or guides to future action.

So what is *The Rime of the Ancient Mariner* then? Some have maintained that it is an attempt to befuddle the reader with a welter of strange evidence and contradictory interpretations, that it is an elaborate *tour de force* of mystification. This account of the poem casts Coleridge in the role of Milton's Satan, who continually changes shape to lure men to their doom. But it might be said that perhaps no other writer in English worries more concertedly than Coleridge about deluding his readers. One almost hears him saying, "My intentions are good, how can I be misunderstood?" And this discomfort at the possibility of being misunderstood perhaps accounts for the peculiar procedure of stratifying his lay sermons for preselected audiences (*The Statesman's Manual* was "addressed to the higher classes of society"; *A Lay Sermon* was to "the higher and middle classes"; and a projected third lay sermon was to have been directed to "the lower and labouring classes of society"). Even his critique (in *Biographia Literaria*, chap. 17) of the theories of poetic diction that Wordsworth expounded in the two Prefaces to *Lyrical Ballads* (and in the Appendix of 1802) involves primarily an argument against the confusions that might arise from importing a "natural" language that would appear strikingly "unnatural" to the audience for poetry. Wordsworth did not really mean what he said about imitating the language of the lower and rustic classes of society, Coleridge insists, because a rustic's language, "purified from all provincialism and grossness, and so far reconstructed as to be made consistent with the rules of grammar" is really a version of the philosophic and ideal language to which all poets and all readers of poetry are accustomed. Coleridge, as he says repeatedly, would be understood.

Why is it, then, that Coleridge is so monumentally difficult to understand? Not only poems like the *Rime*, "Kubla Khan," and "Christabel," but also Coleridge's various prose works continually frustrate many readers who struggle to understand what, exactly, he is saying. And this is a particular problem because Coleridge is continually presented to us as important primarily because of his distinctions—between virtue and vice, symbol and allegory, imagination and fancy. Barbauld-like critics of the *Rime* separate good from evil, and I. A. Richards separates the good (the imagination) from the not-so-good (the fancy). What is it that they know that we don't know?

It may be useful here to turn to the *Biographia Literaria* because it provides the most explicit account of Coleridge's experience and views of reading (and of the ways in which reading involves one's entire set of beliefs about the world). Chapter 12 is named "A Chapter of requests and premonitions concerning the perusal or omission of the chapter that follows." And Coleridge begins it with the following remarks on his reading:

> [In reading philosophical works, I have made the following resolve] *"until you understand a writer's ignorance, presume yourself ignorant of his understanding."* This *golden rule* of mine does, I own, resemble those of Pythagoras in its obscurity rather than its depth. . . . [But the reader] will find its meaning fully explained by the following instances. I have now before me a treatise of a religious fanatic, full of dreams and supernatural *experiences*. I see clearly the writer's grounds, and their hollowness. I have a complete insight into the causes, which through the medium of his body has [sic] acted on his mind; and by application of received and ascertained laws I can satisfactorily explain to my own reason all the strange incidents, which the writer records of himself. And this I can do without suspecting him of any intentional falsehood. . . . I UNDERSTAND HIS IGNORANCE.
>
> On the other hand, I have been re-perusing with the best energies of my mind the Timaeus of PLATO. Whatever I comprehend, impresses me with a reverential sense of the author's genius; but there is a considerable portion of the work, to which I can attach no consistent meaning. . . . I have no insight into the possibility of a man so eminently wise using words with such half-meanings to himself, as must perforce pass into nomeaning to his readers. . . . Therefore, utterly baffled in all my attempts to understand the ignorance of Plato, I CONCLUDE MYSELF IGNORANT OF HIS UNDERSTANDING.

Although Coleridge later speaks of the "organic unity" of this chapter, that "golden rule" of his turns the problem of reading from the text (or the writer) to the reader. For Coleridge's "tolerance" for the ignorant writer—in refusing to suspect him of "any intentional falsehood"—exculpates that writer by turning the reader's own prejudices into a self-reinforcing standard of judgment. No knowledge or virtue or imagination on the part of the author, from this perspective, is susceptible of revealing itself to a reader who does not already believe that such qualities inhere in the work. And the curiosity of the piece is that explanation is fullest (even including physiological causation) when Coleridge describes himself reading a book that he had dismissed before he ever began to read. "Understanding ignorance" and being "ignorant of an author's understanding" are merely techniques through which a reader adjusts his demands to accord with his beliefs.

Such beliefs or prejudices are inevitable, unless, as Coleridge says, we discover "the art of destroying the memory *a parte post*, without injury to its future operations, and without detriment to the judgement." Now Coleridge described his project in *Lyrical Ballads* as that of writing on "supernatural" subjects "so as to transfer from our inward nature a human interest and a semblance of truth sufficient to . . . [produce] that willing suspension of disbelief for the moment, which constitutes poetic faith." But, after all that we have been saying Coleridge said, how is such a "suspension of disbelief" possible? Disbelief is merely a subset of belief, a kind of belief that a thing is not (to paraphrase Gulliver). And the most famous chapter of the *Biographia Literaria*, chapter 13, "On the imagination, or esemplastic power," reveals this process as well as anything in Coleridge's work. Let us start from the end—the distinction between imagination and fancy—to which Coleridge has, he says, been building through the entire book. The secondary imagination idealizes and unifies in its processes of *vital* understanding. The fancy is merely a mechanical and associationist operation that can only rearrange fixities and definites. At some moments Coleridge uses these terms as classificatory, and for I. A. Richards they seem to be universally applicable categories. Richards, for instance, quotes four lines of *Annus Mirabilis* and remarks, "To attempt to read this in the mode of Imagination would be to experiment in mania. . . ." And then he generalizes that in "prose fiction, the detective novel is a type of Fancy, but any presentation of an integral view of life will take the structure of Imagination."

But various other elements of Coleridge's chapter would seem to cast doubt on projects like Richards' *Coleridge on Imagination* and *Practical Criticism* and their assumption that one man's "imagination" is the same as another's. For the letter that Coleridge inserts immediately before the famous distinction is (fictitiously) a letter from a friend "whose practical judgment [Coleridge had] had ample reason to estimate and revere." And although the friend admits that he may not fully understand Coleridge's chapter on imagination, he continually suggests that Coleridge is guilty of breach of promise—for instance, he cites the *Biographia Literaria*'s subtitle, "Biographical Sketches of My Literary Life and Opinions," to argue that it does not lead the reader to anticipate Coleridge's arcane speculations in the *Biographia Literaria*. But the rather major difficulty here is that Coleridge's chapter must do battle with the accumulated expectations of the friend's lifetime: "Your opinions and method of argument were not only so new to me, but so directly the reverse of all I had ever been accustomed to consider as truth." Once again, we are left with a question about the nature of the text (in this case, a deleted or unwritten text): Is the "deficiency" in the text or in the reader?

It seems that a reader can only read the texts that say what he already knows. Thus, the editor of the Gloss reads a text that he knows, while the no-moral critics read a text that they know. And the difficulty is that for Coleridge what you know and what you read are part of a moral dilemma, because one can only act on the basis of what one knows (i. e., believes) and vice is merely the result of incomplete information. Coleridge says in *The Friend* (Essay 14) that "virtue would not be virtue, could it be *given* by one fellow-creature to another" (italics his). In other words, a man must be virtuous to understand the understanding of anyone else's knowledge— and thus to be virtuous.

And if this situation seems to present us with an impasse, it may perhaps explain why Coleridge so desperately wanted to write a summa or *Omniana*, a book of universal knowledge. He continually quotes from an incredibly diverse collection of texts, makes one statement only to confound it with the next, and he even plagiarizes. Many readers feel imposed upon by what they take to be Coleridge's efforts to delude them with airy nothings and falsehoods; and Norman Fruman is merely the latest in the line of critics who "expose" the "scandal" of Coleridge's plagiarisms. But both the plagiarism and the voracious reading perhaps point to related ends: If you are what you read, plagiarism (in a more or less obvious form) becomes inevitable; and if insufficient knowledge or reading is the cause of moral inadequacy, then nothing less than all knowledge—everything—will suffice. Coleridge, like Leibnitz, would "explain and collect the fragments of truth scattered through systems apparently the most incongruous." But like so many of Coleridge's projects, the summa was never completed, because incomplete information (as Coleridge recognized) was not the problem. The problem, rather, was that he could sort information from knowledge, delusion from truth, with no more certainty than anyone else who has lived long enough to have a memory and, thus, prejudice. He said, in the *Aids to Reflection*, that "original sin is not hereditary sin; it is original with the sinner and is of his will." And for Coleridge this original sin was interpretation from a limited perspective that had disproportionate consequences, for the peril was that any apparent extension or reversal might, always, be merely a disguised entrenchment of that particular limitation or prejudice. The Ancient Mariner's redemption or conversion, we are told, occurs when he blesses the sea snakes. But if it seem like a conversion for a man who killed a rather appealing bird to see beauty in snakes, there is also room for a different interpretation. The bird is spoken of in part 5 of the poem as something of a Christ figure, and we all know about the spiritual connotations of snakes. The Mariner's conversion, then, may be a redemption, or, merely a deluded capitulation to the devil. For Coleridge, as for the Ancient Mariner, the problem is that one cannot know better even about whether or not one is knowing better.

The Marginal Gloss

Lawrence Lipking

Marginalia—traces left in a book—are wayward in their very nature; they spring up spontaneously around a text unaware of their presence. Nor could they have been considered publishable until the Romantic period had encouraged a taste for fragments and impulses, the suggestive part rather than the ordered whole. Significantly the term was introduced by Coleridge, that great master of the fragment; and Poe himself (so far as I can find) was the first author ever to publish his marginalia. The charm of such notes depends on their being on the edge: the borders of intelligibility (Poe) or consciousness (Valéry). The reader catches an author off his guard, intercepting a thought that may scarcely have risen to formulation. At their best, marginalia can haunt us like a few passing words overheard in the street; all the more precious because the context remains unknown.

The marginal gloss, however, responds to another frame of mind: the mind to spell everything out. Once glosses explained or interpreted hard words. The modern fashion of translation on a page facing the original might be considered the ultimate gloss—every word explained. But the margin can also offer more general conveniences of interpretation. Before the development of printed books, margins often supplied the information now relegated to the table of contents and index. Anyone who has read a scroll, or a modern microfilm, will appreciate the difficulty of turning back or ahead to locate the right place in the text. The gloss can provide a series of running heads, where the reader's eye, skimming down the page, quickly

From *Critical Inquiry* 3, no. 4 (Summer 1977). © 1977 by The University of Chicago.

grasps the drift of the argument without its details; textbooks still use this device. Unlike marginalia, therefore, the marginal gloss frequently serves to affirm the relation of the part to the whole. Thus Valéry reshapes the chance remarks of Poe into coherent essays. However dense the text, the gloss holds out the hope that all perplexities can be explained and all obliquities reduced to order. Margins, so conceived, rationalize the white space of books. The possibility of glossing demonstrates that the space surrounding print is not a vacuum but a plenum.

II

The need of relating part to whole, in all probability, was the issue that motivated the most famous marginal gloss in English. From the very beginning, the parts of *The Ancient Mariner* appeared to Coleridge as something given. His friend Cruikshank gave him the dream of the skeleton ship; Wordsworth gave him some of the incidents and details; and his reading, as Lowes showed so thoroughly, gave him a ready supply of images and phrases. *The Ancient Mariner* is assembled with the economy of a dream, where fragments of the day return in strange new constellations. But from the first it was never clear to readers that the pieces of the ballad held together. Even Wordsworth, Coleridge's dear collaborator, obviously agreed with the critics that the parts had mastered the whole. In the notorious note he supplied for the second edition of *Lyrical Ballads* (1800), Wordsworth listed among the "great defects" of the poem, "that the events having no necessary connection do not produce each other; and . . . that the imagery is somewhat too laboriously accumulated." Coleridge's poetic career, it might be argued, never fully recovered from the shock of this rejection. If his best poem had been accumulated rather than connected, what right had he to consider himself one of those supreme reconcilers, unifiers, harmonizers: a poet? To answer Wordsworth's criticism, Coleridge would have to demonstrate that the brilliant fragments of *The Ancient Mariner* made one great whole—even if the demonstration obliged him to redefine the nature of poetry itself.

The most ambitious of all Coleridge's critical statements, in fact, literally ends with *The Ancient Mariner*. At the close of the first volume of *Biographia Literaria*, the celebrated passage on the primary and secondary imagination is followed by a promise to explain the powers of the imagination more fully "in the critical essay on the uses of the Supernatural in poetry, and the principles that regulate its introduction: which the reader will find prefixed to the poem of *The Ancient Mariner*." The essay never appeared, of course. But almost simultaneously with the *Biographia* an extraordinary new version of *The Ancient Mariner* came out in *Sibylline Leaves*—the version that we know today. For the first time the strange and seemingly arbitrary happenings of the ballad were interpreted by a civilized scholastic voice: a marginal gloss.

> An ancient Mariner meeteth three Gallants bidden to a wedding-feast, and detaineth one.

It is an ancient Mariner,
And he stoppeth one of three.
"By thy long grey beard and glittering eye,
Now wherefore stopp'st thou me?"

The gloss casts an entirely new light—a kind of secondary imagination—over the poem. The reader who had turned to the first pages of *Lyrical Ballads* in 1798, on the contrary, had been purposely cast adrift. *The Rime of the Ancyent Marinere* opens a book whose title is an oxymoron, whose author is anonymous, and whose archaic language and action, like Chatterton's, seem to suggest a hoax. In one respect, indeed, travesty *does* dominate the poem: a travesty of conversation. The mariner manages to talk to the wedding-guest only by mesmerizing him; no response is allowed; throughout the crisis of the poem the parched tongues of the shipmates do not permit them to speak; and the discourtesy of the idiom extends even to the two voices that discuss the Mariner, in the air and in his soul, as if he were not there. Such impoliteness begins with the first word, which points rather than describes. "It" is a phantom reference, of course, and in the natural world the "it" would be a "he." "Three," moreover, might be three of anything; and the wedding-guest's reasonable question about why he has been stopped will be answered only by a palpable non sequitur, "There was a ship." Coleridge, in 1798, does not encourage the cause and effect, the give and take, of conversation. He deals instead with isolated spirits: the Marinere; the wedding-guest; the poet; and the reader.

In 1817, however, the situation has changed. Now the abrupt opening stanza no longer requires an effort of reading merely to understand what is happening. The gloss briskly ignores "it" to get on with the story, and delivers a commonsense world of ordinary occasions. The word "Gallants" not only tells us something about the dress and social class of the "three," but implies a judgment upon them. Whether we read the gloss or ballad first, moreover, we are always aware of a companion who knows the answers. The activity of the reader's eye, skipping back and forth between the margin and the text, now performs the work once left to the imagination. The gloss familiarizes every supernatural event; it assures us, in spite of the wedding-guest's fears, that the mariner is alive, sustained by a world of facts.

Nor does the gloss confine itself to facts. Again and again it interprets the narrative by reading it as a parable. In the world of the gloss, actions have causes and consequences, parts fit into wholes, and human motives are not arbitrary.

> And lo! the Albatross proveth a bird of good omen, and followeth the ship as it returned northward through fog and floating ice.
>
> And a good south wind sprung up behind;
> The Albatross did follow,
> And every day, for food or play,
> Came to the Mariner's hollo!
>
> In mist or cloud, on mast or shroud,
> It perch'd for vespers nine;
> Whiles all the night, through fog-smoke white,
> Glimmered the white Moon-shine.
>
> The ancient Mariner inhospitably killeth the pious bird of good omen.
>
> "God save thee, ancient Mariner!
> From the fiends, that plague thee thus!—
> Why look'st thou so?"—With my cross-bow
> I shot the ALBATROSS.

The connection between the coming of the albatross and the splitting of the ice, which the ballad had left us to assume, the marginal voice insists upon as "proved." A moment later, therefore, the mariner's crucially unmotivated shooting of the albatross can be judged a recognizable "crime" (as the gloss will call it), a clear violation of the laws of hospitality and piety. Meanwhile, the text's curiously strong association of the bird with moonshine is omitted for the more prosaic nautical detail of "floating ice." The contrast here between the symbolic drama of the text, where everything is to be inferred (" 'Why look'st thou so?' "), and the pious certainty of the commentary could hardly be more pronounced. The gloss is superbly— some might say smugly—knowing. Not in thrall to the mariner's perspective, it understands the meaning of his experiences, it understands him as he cannot understand himself.

Above all, the author of the gloss knows that the world makes sense. A learned occultist, he seems able to answer most of those difficult questions about the nature of Invisible Beings that Thomas Burnet had once posed, in a passage Coleridge chose as an epigraph for *The Ancient Mariner*. When the corpses of the crew are reanimated, for instance, the gloss firmly distinguishes one spirit from another: "But not by the souls of the men, nor by daemons of earth or middle air, but by a blessed troop of angelic spirits, sent down by the invocation of the guardian saint." Appearances cannot mislead the marginal commentator; he perceives, in whatever happens, the signs of a universal order.

At one moment, indeed, this ability amounts to a stroke of genius. When the mariner reaches his lowest point, in part 4, "Alone, alone, all all alone, / Alone on a wide wide sea!," unable to pray and longing to die, he opens his eyes and notices a world outside himself.

> In his lone-
> liness and
> fixedness he
> yearneth to-
> wards the
> journeying
> Moon, and the
> stars that still
> sojourn, yet
> still move
> onward; and
> every where
> the blue sky
> belongs to
> them, and is
> their appointed rest, and their native country and their own natural homes,
> which they enter unannounced, as lords that are certainly expected and yet
> there is a silent joy at their arrival.

> The moving Moon went up the sky,
> And no where did abide:
> Softly she was going up,
> And a star or two beside—
>
> Her beams bemocked the sultry main,
> Like April hoar-frost spread;
> But where the ship's huge shadow lay,
> The charméd water burnt alway
> A still and awful red.

The first stanza by itself, we might suppose, merely confirms the mariner's loneliness. He compares himself to the restless moon; her tranquillity, her companions throw a sad light on his own agonized isolation. But the gloss sees much further. Rather than a commentary, it supplies an extended meditation on the implications of "moving" and "abiding." The mariner, though fixed, can find no place of rest; the moon and stars, though always moving, are always at home. Nature, which through so much of the ballad seems inhabited by unpredictable terrors here takes on another aspect: its motions are appointed, its silence full of joy. By beautifully humanizing the heavens, the gloss suggests a transition to the mariner's impulse of human love for the water snakes—"By the light of the Moon he beholdeth God's creatures of the great calm"—which begins to break the spell, and returns him to the world of the living. The voice in the margin knows that the world is not a collection of individuals but a family. It pronounces a blessing on the interconnectedness of things that confers even on a lonely man the sense of blessing.

But whose voice is speaking in the gloss? Technically, of course, it cannot belong to the poet, since the "eth" and the pious idiom recall another era. Coleridge borrowed his model, in fact, from Renaissance travel books, especially those of Purchas. As the early travellers report their immediate, often confused experiences, which Purchas' gloss relates to other sources, so *The Ancient Mariner* recounts a wild voyage that a gloss restores to context; the margin brings the truth of the voyage home. Coleridge deliberately contrasts the primitive wonderworking of the ballad with a later and wiser reader skilled in hermetic doctrine. And the effect of the contrast is not to explain away the wonders of the poem but to color them with another kind of faith.

Consider, for instance, the reference to the homecoming of "lords" in the gloss on the journeying moon. The charm of the passage, its special poignance, depends on its evocation of a vanished ancestral age, when well-loved lords ruled over well-appointed demesnes. Those days are gone. By the time that Coleridge wrote the gloss, his own early dream of presiding over a happy home had long been dead; his sojourns did not end with silent joy. Yet no one loves his native country so much as an exile. The serene distance of olden times, like the distance of the moon and stars, invests the gloss with an aura of unproblematical faith, of certain knowledge, that can pierce the heart of a reader less sure where he belongs.

Coleridge himself was such a reader. Returning to *The Ancient Mariner* many years after its composition, he must have continued to feel its strange imaginative authority. But the metaphysician in Coleridge could not be satisfied without discovering the principles of that authority: moral, rational, poetic. Both Coleridge's religion and his pride as a poet demanded justification of the realm of spirits. He must learn to read his poem soberly, as Purchas or Burnet might, without the intoxication of creative enthusiasm. And a great deal of the poet's activity, in the decades after *The Ancient Mariner*, may be seen as an effort to become that voice in the gloss: a pious reader entirely at home with his world and his text.

Should such a reader, however, be allowed to intrude on the poem? The terrible power of *The Ancient Mariner*, after all, grows from its sense of isolation. The reader's own loneliness bears witness to the truth of the mariner's experience; the "semblance of truth" transferred from "our inward nature" to procure "a willing suspension of disbelief" is the fearful knowledge that each of us exists alone. The ultimate implication of such knowledge seemed, to many early readers, literally unspeakable; beyond any gloss.

> O Wedding-Guest! this soul hath been
> Alone on a wide wide sea:
> So lonely 'twas, that God himself
> Scarce seemed there to be.

The mariner learns better; but he could not tell his tale at all, he could not mesmerize his hearer, if the "horrible penance" of loneliness did not continue to haunt his vision. To superimpose a pious moral or the illusion of conversation upon such a tale—to gloss it over—is to reduce it to the level of the ordinary. Was the addition of the gloss a mistake?

Doubtless some readers will always think so; and anyone who puts the highest value on spontaneity and excitement will still do well to go back to *Lyrical Ballads* 1798. But Coleridge's own theory requires a different answer. Indeed, according to one of his most important definitions, only on its appearance in *Sibylline Leaves* did *The Ancient Mariner* become a legitimate poem. In the same crucial fourteenth chapter of the *Biographia*, where Coleridge defends *Lyrical Ballads* against its critics, he appeals to the basic nature of poetry. A just poem, he says, does not consist of a "series of striking lines or distiches, each of which, absorbing the whole attention of the reader to itself, disjoins it from its context, and makes it a separate whole, instead of an harmonizing part." But neither does a poem resemble "an unsustained composition, from which the reader collects rapidly the general result, unattracted by the component parts," like a marginal gloss. Rather, Coleridge writes in one of his most brilliant and characteristic passages,

> The reader should be carried forward, not merely or chiefly by the mechanical impulse of curiosity, or by a restless desire to arrive at the final solution; but by the pleasurable activity of mind excited by the attractions of the journey itself. Like the motion of a serpent, which the Egyptians made the emblem of intellectual power; or like the path of sound through the air; at every step he pauses and half recedes, and from the retrogressive movement collects the force which again carries him onward.

The ideal reading of the ideal poem, according to this definition, requires a perpetual advance and retreat, a constant adjustment of the part to the whole. A reader, sharing the perspective of both moon and mariner, has the experience at once of moving and being suspended. It is an experience not unlike reading a ballad of wonders with a marginal gloss.

In its final version, then, *The Ancient Mariner* comes close to defining Coleridge's idea of a poem. The metaphor of the journey, where the succession of strange parts turns out to have been a passage home, demonstrates the internal connection that so many unfriendly reviewers had resolved to overlook. Indeed, Coleridge had found a way of physically involving his critics with his argument. The tension between the two ways of construing the mariner's tale—between experiencing it and interpreting it—is recreated by the eye of every reader, as it snakes back and forth between the text and the margin, interrupting and interpenetrating one script with another, and striving to make a simultaneous order out of two different phases of seeing. Shocking incidents alternate with grave reflections, and the reader tosses between them. Yet finally the ballad and gloss conclude together; for the mariner's own last understanding of his story, the need to love and reverence all things for the sake of that God who "made and loveth all," is identical with the last statement in the margin. As a divided consciousness might be healed by a moment of prayer, so a divided text is healed by a moral intelligible to the wise and simple heart alike. And the reader joins in that union. No longer stunned by wonders, he should rise from the ordeal of this serpentine text exhausted, perhaps, but sadder and wiser.

Coleridge and the Ancestral Voices

Leslie Brisman

Coleridge's greatest triumph against Porlockian intrusion is *The Rime of the Ancient Mariner*. The planned division of labor between Coleridge and Wordsworth for the *Lyrical Ballads* may be thought to leave the Porlock battles behind, but the supernatural is of interest specifically as a counter to the natural, as a way of redeeming nature into imagination. The antiquing of the poem, first in spelling, later through the gloss, may be said to preempt authority for the more-than-natural voice. By themselves, such devices can no more overcome Porlock than can hanging up an old-fashioned knocker keep that spirit of contemporaneity from one's doorstep. Indeed, Porlock does not have to be kept out; he needs to be acknowledged, delineated, and exorcised. I would like to argue that this struggle is to a large extent the subject of the poem. If *The Rime of the Ancient Mariner* is a poem of "pure Imagination," it must achieve that purity as a higher innocence—not an ignorance but a defeat of the person of Porlock. As a poem of imagination it must be concerned with origination, and must come to some sense of its own voice as being more "original," anterior and higher to the genial, natural accents of Porlock. If imagination as a power of origination is the goal, imagination as a "reconciling and mediating power" is the medium in which the struggle takes place.

In its original stasis, the icebound ship marks the fixity of the material— what Blake would call the Ulro—world. Raphael's vision of a greener world

From *Romantic Origins.* © 1978 by Cornell University. Cornell University Press, 1978.

contained within it the energy of sublimation to the Spirit of Origins, the One Almighty "from whom / All things proceed":

> Flowers and their fruit,
> Man's nourishment, by gradual scale sublim'd,
> To vital spirits aspire.

The icebound Arctic knows no such aspiration. Far from reconciling the men on the ship to other living things, or mediating between a natural and a supernatural realm, the ice "all between" is a synecdoche for the solid material world unsublimed to vital spirit; far from a sense of voice, of higher spirit interfusing a lower hemisphere with the breath of the Word, this world is marked with the meaningless sounds of matter chafing against matter. The ice "cracked and growled, and roared and howled." Into this unmediated world of nature comes a spirit of mediation: "at length did cross an Albatross," in a line whose internal rhyme emphasizes the crossing between two realms, the Christ-like nature of the intervention. Not itself the polar spirit—which we can interpret not only as the spirit of the pole but the spirit of polarity—the albatross is rather an emissary, a sign of the relationship between realms. The spirit world mingles with the natural world, creating the kind of "interpenetration of the counteracting powers" Coleridge talks about in the *Biographia* before Porlock cuts him off. "As if it had been a Christian soul, / We hailed it in God's name." The change from ice noises to hailing marks the change to interchange, communication between realms, between beings. The communion is symbolized by this not-of-this-world bird eating "the food it ne'er had eat," what the earlier version specifies as "biscuit worms." It is less the worm than the biscuit that marks the mystery here, for what seems new and remarkable is the mingling of something from the human, commonplace world with something wholly other. Language mediates, in the interchange, and the bird, "every day, for food or play, / Came to the mariner's hollo." This communion, like the "mingled measure" of "Kubla Khan," describes an imaginative paradise, broken by an act that is pure Porlock: "with my crossbow / I shot the albatross."

There is no elaboration, no motivation for the shooting of the albatross, and one does Coleridge wrong to try to turn his tale into a Miltonic account of the story of the fall. Coleridge is not swerving from Milton; he is moving back to a more original relation with the powers behind the story of *Paradise Lost*. The albatross crosses and mediates, the mariner with his crossbow denies that mediation; that is all. Though he wanted to write an epic on the origin of evil, this poem aborts, and in fact fulfills, that desire. Extensity would not do, for it would deflect into story what Coleridge, coming after Milton, desires to restore to an original brevity and simplicity. The resultant poem is about Original Sin in the sense of "original" that interested Coleridge: "A sin is an evil which has its ground or origin in the agent, and not in the compulsion of circumstances." To return the sense of "original" as prehistorical to the sense of "original" 'as belonging wholly to the paradigmatic agent—that would be to approach origins the way a poet can. Coleridge suggests how to read his poem by himself abstracting from the Bible and Milton an Eden story that forms a psychological paradigm. "Milton asserted the will, but declared for the enslavement of the will by an act of the will itself." If Milton is understood to have done that, what more could Coleridge do? In *The Rime* he sets about further reducing the "compulsion of circumstances" into "an act of the will itself."

If the mariner has no "character," as Wordsworth thought, if the mariner's act seems abstracted from a particular person into an idea of personality, it is because Coleridge has further emptied the old tale of all but its essential truth, and is presenting his version as more essentially true:

> In its utmost abstraction and consequent state of reprobation, the will becomes Satanic pride and rebellious self-idolatry in the relations of the spirit to itself, and remorseless despotism relatively to others; the more hopeless as the more obdurate by its subjugation of sensual impulses, by its superiority to toil and pain and pleasure; in short, by the fearful resolve to find in itself alone the one absolute motive of action, under which all other motives from within and from without must be either subordinated or crushed.

This seems to me appropriate in idea, though perhaps inappropriate in size. Tacking it on *The Rime* may be like hanging an albatross around the mariner's neck. The weightiness of the moral was a problem of which Coleridge was aware, but we do him wrong to exaggerate it. Porlock, after all, is an enlightener, one who would clear the air of these huge flappings on metaphysical wings. We need only the sense that the shooting of the albatross is an act of will, and that this "enlightenment" breaks the spell that bound nature and supernature in mysterious communion.

Immediately we are confronted in the poem with the sun, emblem of the tyranny of the natural world, and with the loss in language, the medium of exchange between worlds. Linguistic repetition mocks the stasis, the failure in the transaction that language could perform. In a stanza that repeats but negates the earlier description we find that no bird comes to the mariner's hollo. The voices of the mariners are equally disjointed. First they aver that a hellish thing was done: "for all averred, I had killed the bird / That made the breeze to blow." When the sun rises, "all averred, I had killed the bird / That brought the fog and mist." Language, and with it moral judgment, is now tied to the weather, that most Ulro of topics of conversation. If the weather is not to be the most "natural" of things in this poem, the usurpation of nature by the forces of the supernatural is prepared by the collapse of language as the communication between realms.

It is often pointed out that the mariner remains passive through most of the poem. After the shooting of the albatross, the first action he takes is a startlingly willful counteraction to the linguistic blight. "Through utter drought all dumb we stood! / I bit my arm, I sucked the blood, / And cried, A sail! a sail!" Again, one may be adding further weight round the mariner's neck in noting that this bloodsucking is a perversion of the communion the albatross brought. But the linguistic events of the poem are so few and so startling that they cry out to be thus invested. Perhaps the burden can be legitimately shifted from critic to mariner here, for in the story he makes this sole and feeble attempt to take salvation in his own hands, to make the restoration of language a restoration of communion. But beyond his single act, the whole of part 3 of the poem may be read as the will's effort at imaginative restoration.

If shooting the albatross is the Porlockian act that breaks the relation between realms, we must get back to the *tertium aliquid* Coleridge was talking about in the *Biographia* before the break there. Building this intermediate state is the work of the imagination, and the vagueness of perception at the beginning of part 3 is an imitation of that labor. The mariner beholds "a something in the sky," where the "somethingness" marks a step in the direction of imagination. Coleridge writes of the "middle state of mind" being the state of imagination, for the mind must be left "hovering between images":

> As soon as it is fixed on one image, it becomes understanding; but while it is unfixed and wavering between them, attaching itself permanently to none, it is imagination. Such is the fine description of Death in Milton:
>
> The other Shape,
> If Shape it might be call'd, that shape had none
> Distinguishable in member, joint, or limb,
> Or substance might be call'd, that shadow seem'd,
> For each seem'd either; black it stood as night;

> Fierce as ten furies, terrible as hell,
> And shook a dreadful dart: what seem'd his head
> The likeness of a kingly crown had on.

In light of Coleridge's phrase, "as soon as it is fixed on one image, it becomes understanding," we may call to mind Porlock's position on the reason and understanding, his desire to "enlighten" the mystery of Reason by bringing things down to his level of understanding. It is curious that the Porlock of the *Biographia* expresses confusion at Coleridge's terms by citing the same Miltonic passage:

> In short, what I had supposed substances were thinned away into shadows, while everywhere shadows were deepened into substances:
>
> > If substance might be call'd that shadow seem'd,
> > For each seem'd either!

Porlock, after all, is a friend, and what he wants to do in the *Biographia* is turn the philosophic discussion into a literary *event*, one more happening in an essentially naturalistic narrative. This is not unimaginative but primitively imaginative. It does establish its own indefinite, its own *tertium aliquid*, only failing to recognize the distinction between matters of the spirit and those of the will. *The Rime* is not spoiled by the weight of its moral because the battle over the will is not the mariner's but the poet's. Part 3 of the poem does have the mariner bite his arm, but the narrative that follows is not due to some willful imagining on his part; it is due to the poet's attempt to write "willfully," to his effort to write the kind of poetry that represents imagination not yet freed from the demands of the will. The section ends with the souls of the shipmates flying away: "and every soul, it passed me by, / Like the whizz of my cross-bow." Each death is a departure of spirit, one more emblem of the break in mediation between realms. It is as if the original act of will were in the air, haunting the events of this part of the poem.

What takes place in the encounter with the ghost ship is a willed imagining, an attempt by the poet to mediate again, to turn definite into indefinite in the manner of the passage Coleridge cites from Milton. The confusion between shadow and substance, Coleridge argues, allows for the imagination in a way that no fixed sketch or skeleton figure could. Like Milton's two indefinites are Coleridge's: "Is that a Death? and are there two? / Is Death that woman's mate?" The surprise here is the mariner's, but we can read the description as a two-willful heightening of dramatic tension. The mariner has further penance to do, and the poem has further to go.

Part 4 puts the problem explicitly in terms of communication: the mariner cannot pray. For shooting a bird, the resulting dumbness and isolation is too disproportionate a punishment by any standard. But if we interpret the shooting as a Porlockian interruption, we can read what follows less as expiation for a crime than as education of desire. Porlock has to be arrested so that he can be made to confront the undisturbed "one life" that it is his nature to interrupt. The vision of unity in part 4, from water snakes up to the moon, is a vision of the continuity of body and spirit, pure and impure, motion and stasis, permanence and flux. Fixed in the still sea, fixated by the stare of his shipmates, Porlock is less punished than he is awed.

In a gesture that itself indicates a restoration of communication between realms, Coleridge provides the most beautiful description as the gloss:

> In his loneliness and fixedness he yearneth towards the journey-ing Moon, and the stars that still sojourn, yet still move onward; and every where the blue sky belongs to them, and is their appointed rest, and their native country and their own natural homes, which they enter unannounced, as lords that are certainly expected and yet there is a silent joy at their arrival.

There is more of Raphael's speech, there is more of Milton here than perhaps anywhere in Coleridge's verse. The stars that "still sojourn, yet still move onward" express the reconciliation between motion and stasis, matter and spirit, that marks the original place in vision from which Coleridge was rapt by recalling himself in Lycidas-like interruption. The paradox of so-journing while moving, if one can use so harsh a term for so gentle a moment, is like the oxymorons that prompted Coleridge to turn to Milton to illustrate the way imagination is kept suspended, kept from falling into understanding. Then comes the seemingly gratuitous comparison, whose excess is like grace, in which the stars are lords. Language is heightened to the point where "native country" and "natural homes" are not terms of intrusion into a spiritual realm but marks of the perfect peace, the perfect integration of nature perceived as the One Life. Nothing in the realm of nature can be said to correspond to the description of lords "certainly expected," and nothing could be more expressive of this vision of harmony of the natural with the supernatural, united by a power that is imagination itself. There is silent joy at the stars' arrival not from an insufficiency of communication but from perfect plenitude, the fullness of relation of star to sky. The stars enter unannounced, yet we are as far as can be from a sense of intrusion. Here is everything that Porlock is not.

Having been made all eye, the mariner must now bring the vision closer, must come to see his own nature participating in that cosmic nature. In this poem, the moon is imaginative vision, the sun physical or all-too-natural sight. The mariner yearns for the journeying moon that goes up "softly." Then the eye turns from that soft whiteness to the redness closer to the self:

> Her beams bemocked the sultry main,
> Like April hoar-frost spred;
> But where the ship's huge shadow lay
> The charmed water burnt alway
> A still and awful red.

The turn inward is repeated in the following two stanzas. The first is closer to the moon vision, and the mariner beholds the water snakes "in tracks of shining white." Are these actually serpentine creatures, or is he watching the moonlight slithering down wave crescents? The slight ambiguity marks the indefiniteness of imagination not reduced to understanding. The next stanza makes the necessary move closer to the self. The water snakes are observed "within the shadow of the ship," where their beauty overwhelms the mariner. Presumably these are sea creatures, not optical illusions, but this should not deter us from seeing the ship's shadow as the shadow of selfhood, the water snakes as images of serpentine Porlock. The difficult reintegration of the natural man into the One Life is expressed by the visionary difficulty of including even water snakes in the Miltonic continuum of living forms.

On this point we tend to read the poem too glibly, as though all one really needed were love, as though *The Rime* were actualizing Gloucester's invocation:

> Let the superfluous and lust dieted man
> That slaves your ordinance, that will not see
> Because he does not feel, feel your pow'r quickly.

In Coleridge's poem the problem is more a matter of sight preceding feeling. The vision of the journeying moon is a vision of the One Life, in the context of which the water snakes can appear beautiful and evoke the mariner's "spring of love." He had been in something of the state of Coleridge's Dejection Ode:

> All this long eve, so balmy and serene,
> Have I been gazing on the western sky,
> And its peculiar tint of yellow green:
> And still I gaze—and with how blank an eye!
> And those thin clouds above, in flakes and bars,
> That give away their motion to the stars;
> Those stars, that glide behind them or between,
> Now sparkling, now bedimmed, but always seen:
> Yon crescent Moon, as fixed as if it grew
> In its own cloudless, starless lake of blue;
> I see them all so excellently fair,
> I see, not feel, how beautiful they are!

The mariner is made to see, then to feel. The "blank eye" of the Dejection Ode, the Gloucester eye, the Porlock eye, comes to see, and in that seeing to sense a reestablishment of the communion that the Porlockian intervention had denied. I emphasize the order of the progress because Porlock, who suffers from a failure of vision, is, in his own terms, loving enough. As the natural will, Porlock must be brought to passivity before the activity of love is regenerated. To see love being generated from vision is to see restored the nature of imagination as the power of origination. Porlock habitually comes too soon. If, as Coleridge remarked about his own fluency, the Porlock voice comes readily, it must be hushed or made to appear belated so that the finer tone can first be heard. The simile of the gloss expresses the "silent joy" in the sky, and that silence, that recognition of the inadequacy of the Porlock voice, precipitates the redemption of the voice: "O happy living things! no tongue / Their beauty might declare."

Seeing what cannot be spoken, the mariner is now able to speak: "A spring of love gushed from my heart, / And I blessed them unaware." The "spring of love" is an original spring, coming up in contrast to the streams, the continuities of nature, in which every act, every impression, derives from its immediate physical causes. "This is the essential character by which *Will* is opposed to Nature, as *Spirit*, and raised above Nature, as *self-determining* Spirit—this namely, that it is a power of *originating* an act or state." At the same time, it seems as if a higher benignity were flowing into him, as if he were now participating in the continuities of spiritual reality. The "unaware" is the slight but full recognition of the suppression of the will, the subordination of one's own power of origination to an inspired one, one that is breathed into the self. Here is Coleridge in *Aids to Reflection*, speaking of the coming together of will and submissiveness in a higher harmony, and using the same metaphor—now literally—of inspiration:

> Will any reflecting man admit that his own Will is the only and sufficient determinant of all he is, and all he does? Is nothing to be attributed to the harmony of the system to which he belongs, and to the pre-established Fitness of the Objects and Agents, known and unknown, that surround him, as acting *on* the will, though doubtless, *with* it likewise? a process, which the co-instantaneous yet reciprocal action of the air and the vital energy of the lungs in breathing may help to render intelligible.
>
> Again in the world we see every where evidence of a Unity, which the component parts are so far from explaining, that they necessarily presuppose it as the cause and condition of their existing *as* those parts.

The mariner perceives the water snakes as part of that Unity, and is impelled to bless them. No longer *ab extra*, he speaks now as part of the continuum of the One Life. Far from interrupting, potency of voice now expresses the continuity of spirit worlds: "Sure my kind saint took pity on me, / And I blessed them unaware." Is it his voice, or some kind saint's working through him? The moment of anti-self-consciousness is the moment of restoration of the relationship between all spirits—in Raphael's phrase—"each in their several active spheres assigned." And the harmony of the spirits' relation is mirrored in the perfect concord of verbal repetition:

> A spring of love gushed from my heart,
> And I blessed them unaware:
> Sure my kind saint took pity on me,
> And I blessed them unaware.

It is as if the single act were approached from both directions in the spiritual world, the human heart reaching up to offer the blessing, the kind saint reaching down, singing the same note, the same poetic line.

The restored relationship of the spiritual world means a restored communion between the levels of spiritual being: "the self-same moment I could pray." What more remains? This is the end of part 4, and the poem is less than half over. The pace of the action changes, as though the poem were approximating the status of the stars that "still sojourn, yet still move onward." With the albatross off, the redemption is sufficiently assured for the poem to afford the tone of sojourning. In terms of the moral action, what follows is more difficult, as though refining the terms the poem has to this point established. No further action from the mariner is required—except that he perceive the poem's further refinement in the conception of the relationship between levels of being. The mariner has been pitied and overwhelmed. If we sense nonetheless that the moment of blessing the water snakes is an imaginative moment, a delicate balance between a giving and a receiving, what remains to be achieved is a firmer sense that one can reestablish relationship from the self upward.

Part 5, first, is a resting place where the mariner is refreshed with rain, where we bask, more generally, in the light of a giving from above. Part 6 will bring a restored vision of the relation of lower to higher voice, but meanwhile the higher spirits take over. The dead rise in silence, emblem of passive relationship to higher authority. In the sole stanza of human community—or what is, rather, an eerie parody of it—the mariner joins his nephew:

> The body of my brother's son
> Stood by me, knee to knee:
> The body and I pulled at one rope,
> But he said nought to me.

The silence is further emphasized in the first version of the poem, which adds the lines, "And I quak'd to think of my own voice / How frightful it would be!" Why would his voice be frightful? A troup of spirits has taken over the others: the mariner too feels "taken over": "I thought that I had died in sleep, / And was a blessed ghost." Could it be his natural voice that would be frightful to a group of spirits, or frightful to be heard in such a spirited atmosphere? Or does he fear his own accents would be more strange, more ghastly than the silence? In either case he remains silent, while "sweet sounds rose slowly through their mouths." These sounds of birds, of brooks, are most welcome, though their beauty cannot obscure their strangeness. (The disorienting effect of displaced sounds of nature is like that effect sometimes used in contemporary cinema at moments of solipsistic stress, or when one person wants to distress another.) The sounds of nature alternate with "angels' song / That makes the heavens be mute," where that muteness, the "quiet tone" that is sung, marks the desired harmony.

These are harmonies of sounds as sounds. Their strangeness at this point in the poem establishes a distinction between sound and voice. Voices of nature from the mouths of spirits express just the achievement, and just the limitation of the achievement, of the voice of blessing (spirit) in the mouth of the mariner (natural man). The danger is that, though the mariner can pray, the sounds will come from the larynx, worked upon by spirits the way an Eolian harp is moved by the winds. Disembodied sounds, like inspirited bodies, can stand not for communication but for a more subtle, more psychically disturbing disjunction between sound and spirit. Voice is sound and stance, and the poem moves on in part 6 to a redemption of the stance, the relationship between sound-maker and sound-receiver.

In the mariner's trance he hears, and in his soul discerns, two voices in the air. The two voices are a kind of abstraction of the problem of voice, but the relation established between them is the one element of communion not yet achieved. What is their relationship? The first is an inquiring, the second a knowing and answering spirit. They are not voices of nature and grace, of a first and second dispensation, although the knowledgeable spirit has the "softer voice, / As soft as honey-dew." The meaning of their encounter may lie in what it means to be an answering voice. The first spirit inquires a second time: "But tell me, tell me! speak again, / Thy soft response renewing." If this is to be a response to a question, it is also the responsiveness of spiritual reality, the harmonious concord of the One Life. The soft, second voice answers the question about the ocean with what Reeve Parker calls a "virtually Shelleyan myth":

> Still as a slave before his lord,
> The ocean hath no blast;
> His great bright eye most silently
> Up to the Moon is cast—
> If he may know which way to go;
> For she guides him smooth or grim.
> See, brother, see! how graciously
> She looketh down on him.

It will take Coleridge's heir to sustain moments like this—visions of an original grace so frequently sought, so often found by Coleridge himself to be just out of sight. "And still I gaze," he complains in the Dejection Ode, "and with how blank an eye!" What is to keep the mariner from this dreariness, or the condition of the blind old man of "Limbo," who "gazes the orb with moon-like countenance" and "seems to gaze at that which seems to gaze on him?" Parker finds that line from "Limbo" a triumphant encounter, but it seems to me to represent the painful sterility—like that the mariner has already experienced—of the quest for romantic origins reduced to semiotics; there is no Emersonian transparency in the Limbo man's "eyeless face all eye" but the blind confrontation of one sign with another, "seems" staring at "seems." In *The Rime*, on the other hand, the

Second Voice apprehends a visionary grace that restores prophetic sight of an originally responsive universe.

What the Second Voice's response about responsiveness means in moral terms is implicit in the master-slave metaphor, "Still as a slave before his lord, / The ocean hath no blast." The moral implication of this metaphor is one Wordsworth inherits in the Intimations Ode; it is also implicit in Gloucester's lines about the man "That slaves your ordinance, that will not see / Because he does not feel." The man who slaves ordinance, who treats the laws that ought to govern the relations between creatures like slaves to be bandied about, must be brought to feel. Because he does not feel love he is made, by an act of poetic justice, to feel power, the force of ordinance. That much has happened to the mariner and is the subject of the prophetic denunciation uttered by Gloucester, who has gained the seer's sententiousness without abandoning his cult of retribution. Returning to a purer morality characteristic of the mythmaker rather than the prophet caught in bad times, Coleridge's Second Voice reveals love to be the basis of the physical and metaphysical universes, governing the attraction of both persons and planets. "Feeling" in the sense of love is equivalent to feeling the force of ordinance—of the Miltonic hierarchical order of spirits. It takes an act of vision to see that this is vision, not simply a triumph of the moral will; but the essence of vision is learning to read not horizontally—perceiving cause and effect, act and albatross—but vertically—perceiving the harmonious relation of lowly to exalted creature, of the subservient spirit to that, in Raphael's terms "more spiritous and pure." From the Second Voice's spatially and morally superior perspective, law is love, though Porlock smirk.

Natural affection is the last stronghold of Porlock, whose greatest pride is that, if he interrupts vision, he yet more deeply feels. This special pride must be put in its special place, and the relationship that is love must come to be seen not as natural man's alternative to vision but as the essence of the visionary relationship between all sentient things. The primacy of the natural voice is Porlock's great claim. If the soft response is not a natural man's denial of vision but a higher vision, more of a vision, then imagination has restored the relationship of origination. The relation of moon to ocean is the relation, in this poem, of the imaginative realm to the natural man, who has not an alternative stance (from which he can take potshots at mediating birds) but one acknowledged position in a ladder of being. The vision of soft response is the vision of hierarchy among all spirits, some of whom are more in voice, are more knowledgeable, are more "sublim'd," in Milton's term, than others. Porlock is like an idiot questioner, whose good-natured skepticism would shake every rung. Blake would cast him out; Coleridge finds instead a voice to answer him—finds instead the image of answering voice to represent the relation of spirit to more elevated spirit, of first to second voice. In the communication of those spirits is restored stance and restored voice.

"The supernatural motion is retarded," and we step back from this vision, from the mariner's trance, into the realm of nature. At last the departing spirits are silenced: "Oh! the silence sank / Like music on my heart." With a sense of enormous relief we reenter human community—hermit, pilot, and boy. But the hierarchy of voices is not destroyed, and the mariner, far from being now a man among men, visits the human community with all the aura of otherness with which the supernatural visited him. The pilot falls into a fit when the mariner moves his lips. The natural interrupter of the supernatural vision becomes the visionary interrupter of the natural. Then (at that point in the story) as now (the dramatic time of the poem) he stoppeth one of three. With "strange power of speech," the mariner assumes his place in the hierarchy of voices, "Each in their several active spheres assign'd, / Till body up to spirit work, in bounds / Proportion'd to each kind." As his business is to help other bodies "up to spirit work," he goes about seeking out the Porlocks, interrupting marriage feasts for whatever increase in vision his power of voice can impart.

How much of an increase in vision is there? The reading I have been arguing for must seem terribly optimistic to anyone heeding the visionary voice of the poem, which trembles with more ominous tones than those taken into account here. Like the ancestral voices of "Kubla Khan," the prophetic tones of *The Rime* prophesy a more difficult relationship with the outside world. Porlock is not to be so easily let in, and to characterize the change in the mariner from an interrupting Porlock to a visionary interrupter of Porlocks may seem too shifty a subterfuge. Yet in a way the poem licenses such naïveté, and if the enlightenment of the wedding guest seems to come too easily, we must realize that such is the nature of enlightenment itself, lightening for the guest, and ultimately for the reader, the burden the mariner has assumed. The moral of the poem is to the visionary experience as the interpretation of the poem is to the text. Moralizers and interpreters are Porlocks. As critics we are knockers on the door, and though we invariably intrude, arguing our way into a text, we hope that our voices will somehow be assimilated into the hierarchy and added to the defense against those whom we see as the attacking outsiders.

Poets, like angelic spirits, have their hierarchies too, and a poet stands in relation to his precursor as a first to a second voice. The ancestral voices were right, predicting war. Porlock must be tackled, not ignored or shown the cottage or Xanadu door. As he grows, the younger poet comes to share rather than interrupt the vision of the more knowing, more softly responding voices. The Dejection Ode comes to declare that one does not steal from oneself all the natural man; the voice of the natural man, "a sweet and potent voice, of its own birth," finds itself not standing apart but participating in a harmony of voices. The individual soul's joy gets to be seen *as* the One Life:

> Joy lift her spirit, joy attune her voice;
> To her may all things live, from pole to pole,
> Their life the eddying of her living soul!

Not cast out, the idiot questioner is rather made to listen, to participate in colloquy that binds spirit to spirit. These are the noncorporeal battles of eternity, fought between each poet-as-Porlock and whatever his "abstruse research" can do to make him an ancestral voice. The battle is a subjective one, but as Coleridge says of Milton, "the Objectivity consists in the universality of its subjectiveness": "In Paradise Lost—indeed in every one of his poems—it is Milton himself whom you see; his Satan, his Adam, his Raphael, almost his Eve—are all John Milton; and it is a sense of this intense egotism that gives me the greatest pleasure in reading Milton's works. The egotism of such a man is a revelation of spirit."

We can say the same of Coleridge when he is fighting the Porlock battles. The victory is not in trammeling the natural man but in finding there the listening ear tuned to the higher harmony. "So I would write," says Coleridge, looking back at Milton, and dreaming of spending twenty years on an epic, "haply not unhearing of that divine and rightly-whispering Voice, which speaks to mighty minds of predestined Garlands, starry and unwithering." Coleridge, haply, was not unhearing of the rightly-whispering Voice, though he did not take years in Miltonic "deep metaphysical researches" preparing to write the great poem. If Coleridge in the Dejection Ode renounces the plan "by abstruse research to steal / From my own nature all the natural man," he nevertheless does find his predestined garland, starry and unwithering.

Acknowledging and arguing with Porlock, Coleridge opens the way, as the gloss says about the stars, to native country and natural home. "They enter unannounced, as lords that are certainly expected and yet there is a silent joy at their arrival." If we keep in mind what a warm, lovable fellow, though a dark, worrisome, and destructive specter this Porlock is, we can picture a gregarious Coleridge opening the door and inviting Porlock in. Porlock interrupts, but since he comes in as the natural man, he polarizes the identity of the poet and makes us see the interrupted bard as a guest already at the party, one of the more original, more inspired company. Commenting on the way man is separated from his contemporaneous (we could say his Porlockian) self, Michel Foucault finds that "amid things that are born in time and no doubt die in time, he, cut off from all origin, is already there." Coleridge the poet is already *there*, preceding and preparing the way for his interrupter and belated successor.

Sexual Personae

Camille Paglia

The supreme male heroine in Coleridge, and probably the most influential one in modern literature, is the protagonist of *The Rime of the Ancient Mariner*. Wordsworth was the first to remark upon the Mariner's passive suffering. In his note to the 1800 edition of *Lyrical Ballads*, Wordsworth speaks of the "great defects" of the poem: "first that the principal person has no distinct character . . . : secondly, that he does not act, but is continually acted upon." Harold Bloom says, "Frequently noted by critics is the extraordinary passivity of the Mariner." Graham Hough equates the ship's motionlessness in the poem with "a complete paralysis of the will." George Whalley goes further in claiming, "The Mariner's passivity is Coleridge's too." My reading of *The Ancient Mariner* takes this passivity as the central psychological fact about the poem. I particularly reject "moral" interpretations typified by a much-admired essay by Robert Penn Warren. Edward E. Bostetter has argued against Warren point by point:

> The poem is the morbidly self-obsessed account of a man who through his act has become the center of universal attention. The supernatural powers who control the world concentrate upon his punishment and redemption. Two hundred men drop dead because of his act. . . . The crew has no identity apart from him. . . . The reader has no awareness of them as human beings; he watches their deaths without surprise and without feeling

except as they affect the Mariner. When, dying, the men fix
their eyes upon the Mariner, the effect is not only to intensify
his sense of guilt but to emphasize his importance.

The Mariner as the "center of universal attention": this perfectly describes
the operatic self-dramatization of the male heroine, a prima donna who
triumphs through exquisite public suffering. The eyes of the universe are
fixed on the ritual victim. The Coleridgean ring of eyes is part paranoiac
rebuke, part eroticizing adoration, part seductive allure. These eyes crucify
the protagonists of Coleridge's great poems by pinning them in petrified
passivity, an uncanny world-fear.

Sagas of the male heroine are always artistically endangered by the
serpentine dynamic of self-identification. The Mariner, with his "long grey
beard" and "skinny hand," recalls those Wordsworthian solitaries with
"grey hairs" and "palsied hands" in whom I have seen a self-identification
by the poet so extreme as to mar the text by eruptions of debilitating
sentimentality. *The Ancient Mariner* is flecked with passages so badly written
as to approach Lewis Carroll parody:

> "Hold off! unhand me, grey-beard loon!"
> Eftsoons his hand dropt he.

> The Wedding-Guest here beat his breast,
> For he heard the loud bassoon.

> Four times fifty living men,
> (and I heard nor sigh nor groan)
> With heavy thump, a lifeless lump,
> They dropped down one by one.

Rhyme has become merely ritualistic chiming, a gathering cloud of fateful
inevitability. Stanzas descend into slapstick and heedlessly sail on. *The
Ancient Mariner* is one of the greatest poems in English literature, one of
the most influential, one of the most unforgettable, and yet what it achieves
is almost in defiance of language. Vision and execution are sometimes wildly
divergent. Coleridge's conversation poems are in consistently better taste,
sober and refined, yet they are minor works in literary history, part of the
prior age of sensibility, and would never have made the poet's fame. A
similar disjunction of form and content affects Coleridge's heir Edgar Allan
Poe. The French accused America of having slighted her greatest poet in
Poe, and it is possible Poe sounds better in Baudelaire's translation than in

English. Poe, like Coleridge, is a giant of imagination, and imagination has its own laws. Coleridge's mystery poems and Poe's short stories are incomparable works of chthonian horror in which the daemonic expresses itself nakedly. Dionysus has always shaken off rules of Apollonian form.

Coleridge and Poe give us visions which transcend language, which belong to the dream-experience which is beyond language. Modern psychoanalysis, particularly in the French school of Lacan, has seriously overestimated the linguistic character of the unconscious. Dreaming is a pagan cinema. The wit of dreams comes from treating words as if they were objects. Freud may have slighted the visual content of dreaming because of his own Jewish bias for the word. Coleridge and Poe have written works of cinema. Had film been available as a medium, perhaps that is the form they would have chosen, for language here is only an obstruction in the instant communication of vision. To evaluate the language of *The Ancient Mariner* by the standards of Renaissance or eighteenth-century English poetry would be depressing. There are few great phrases in it; for example, "And ice, mast-high, came floating by,/As green as emerald." I would assert all such wonderful moments in *The Ancient Mariner* look forward to "Christabel," that "Christabel" with its cold green snake is struggling to be born throughout this poem. The rhetorical weaknesses of *The Ancient Mariner* as well as Poe's tales have been produced by a warp of self-identification. Vision drives with such force from the unconscious that the craftsmanlike shape-making of consciousness cannot keep up and is left lagging behind. *The Ancient Mariner* is a rhapsody of the male heroine, filled with piercing arias:

> Alone, alone, all, all alone,
> Alone on a wide wide sea!
> And never a saint took pity on
> My soul in agony.

Such emotional expressionism is possible in Italian but not in English. "Alone, alone, all, all alone": this sentimental refrain is a *frisson* of masochistic ecstasy. Shakespeare's Richard II declares in his maudlin fall: "And my large kingdom for a little grave,/ A little little grave, an obscure grave" (III.iii.153–54). Intensifications of littleness shrink to a cartoon pinpoint of dancing dwarves. Similarly, Coleridge's intoning alones overpopulate themselves mercilessly, like a canine chorus. The sheer velocity of self-identification has also masked from the poet the infelicity of rhyming "thump" with "lump." Unfortunately, the agrarian comedy rooted in our Anglo-Saxon monosyllables turns such lines into bathos. But there is at work in *The Ancient Mariner* the same ritual principle we observed in "To William Wordsworth": a pagan sexual exhibitionism. The self-pity of *The Ancient Mariner* is like the self-flagellation of the ancient goddess cults. It is neither callow nor neurotic. It is a ritual device to facilitate daemonic vision. The Romantic male heroine is a self-emasculating devotee before the chthonian enormity of nature.

The sexual personae of *The Ancient Mariner* form a pattern of allegory. The poem begins with the Mariner stopping the Wedding-Guest as he enters a marriage banquet. The deep structure of this scene is exactly that of the opening of "Christabel": a stranger with a "glittering eye" puts a spell on an innocent, who falls under daemonic compulsion. The Mariner detains the guest with his tale of woe, which takes up the whole poem. At the end, the guest gloomily turns away from the bridegroom's door and departs; the merry feast goes on without him. My theory is this: the Bridegroom, Wedding-Guest, and Mariner are all aspects of one self, of Coleridge. The Bridegroom is a masculine persona, a self comfortably integrated in society. This virile alter ego is always perceived longingly and at a distance, through an open door through which come bursts of happy laughter. The Wedding-Guest, who is "next of kin" to the Bridegroom, is an adolescent supplicant aspiring to sexual fulfillment and collective joy. To achieve this, the Wedding-Guest must merge with the Bridegroom. But he is always prevented from doing so by the appearance of a spectre self, the Mariner, the male heroine or hermaphroditic self who luxuriates in passive suffering. It's a case of always the bridesmaid and never the bride. The Wedding-Guest turns away at the end because once more the hieratically wounded self has won. The guest will never be the Bridegroom. As many times as he attempts to pass through the door to the place of festivity, the Mariner will materialize and paralyze him with his seductive tale. This doorway is the obsessive scene of the Coleridgean sexual crux. Ostracism and casting out are the Romantic road to identity. Will that doorway ever be breached? Yes, in "Christabel." And only by the most bizarre strategy of perversity and transsexualism.

The apparently pivotal event in the Mariner's tale is the killing of the albatross, from which follow all his sufferings. From the first time I read the poem in high school, I thought the albatross a superficial appendage, a kind of pin-the-tail-on-the-donkey, and I considered the stress on it by teachers and critics unconvincing and moralistic. Long afterward I learned it was Wordsworth who suggested the idea of the albatross to Coleridge, which proves my point. This albatross is the biggest red herring in poetry. Its only pertinence is as a vehicle of transgression. The Mariner commits an obscure crime and becomes the focus of cosmic wrath. But he is as blameless as any of the shadow heroes of Kafka, who are hauled before faceless courts of law. In the world of *The Ancient Mariner* any action is immediately punished. Masculine assertion is rebuked and humanity condemned to suffering passivity. Blake's *Crystal Cabinet* contains a similar dramatic crisis: the moment the male acts, he is expelled into the wilderness. Blake's male is transformed into a "Weeping Babe" in infantile dependency upon a "Weeping Woman." Coleridge's Mariner is also propelled backward into an evilly maternal world. The ship is becalmed:

> The very deep did rot: O Christ!
> That ever this should be!
> Yea, slimy things did crawl with legs
> Upon the slimy sea.

Stasis, slime. This is a vision of primal nondifferentiation, the chthonian swamp of generation. The universe has returned to one big womb, claustrophobic, airless, teeming with monstrous prehuman mud creatures. The Mariner's appeal to Christ is the opposite of what it seems. It shows that Coleridge, despite his conscious commitment to Christianity, understands with the intuition of a great poet that the swamp world of the Great Mother precedes the world of Christ and is ready at any moment to engulf it. That Coleridge specifically visualized a chthonian swamp is suggested by two remarks: he once spoke of the "Sands and Swamps of Evil" and again of lust as "the reek of the Marsh."

The Ancient Mariner is one of Romantic poetry's great regressions to the daemonic and primeval. Every man makes a marine voyage out of that cell of archaic ocean which is the sac of womb-waters. We all emerge covered with slime and gasping for life.

> The many men, so beautiful!
> And they all dead did lie:
> And a thousand thousand slimy things
> Lived on; and so did I.

All hopes for beauty and manhood lie dead. Male power can never surmount female power. Procreative chthonian nature will always have the last word. We live in the slime of our bodies, which hold imagination hostage. Our mother-born bodies are the unregenerate nature which is beyond God's redemption. The "slimy sea" of chthonian nature cancels and nullifies the words of Christ. Coleridge is overwhelmed by a pagan vision which comes to him from below and beyond his own ethics. *The Ancient Mariner* is influenced by the Gothic novel, but it transports its tale out of the historical world of castles and abbeys into the sublime theater of a desolate nature. But expansion of space is just another cul-de-sac. Coleridge brilliantly succeeds in converting the open sea into a rotting sepulchre, which I have called the daemonic womb of Gothic. This is one black hole from which Christ will never rise. *The Ancient Mariner* is the obvious source of Poe's novella *The Narrative of Arthur Gordon Pym*, with its disastrous voyage in a womb- and tomb-bellied ship. Evolution and motion are an illusion in the dank prison space of chthonian nature. This is the ultimate cause of the Coleridgean male heroine's crushing passivity. Mankind staggers under the brutal burden of mother nature.

Language, we have noted, is mutilated for vision in *The Ancient Mariner*. Thus it is appropriate that the naming of gods in the poem has a negative backlash effect. To name the good seems to produce the birth of evil. Invocation of Christ's name fails to release the Mariner from his imprisonment in the nightmare womb of ocean. A sail is sighted on the horizon, and there is a moment of hope and joy. The Mariner attempts a new prayer: "Heaven's Mother send us grace!" But sanctified language is profaned by daemonic revelation. On the ship is the grossest female apparition:

> *Her* lips were red, *her* looks were free,
> Her locks were yellow as gold:
> Her skin was as white as leprosy,
> The Night-mare LIFE-IN-DEATH was she,
> Who thicks man's blood with cold.

Appeals to sky cult are useless. As if irritated by references to her benign successor, the tender Madonna, the ur-mother makes her sensational appearance. She is the Whore of Babylon, the daemon unbound. Her lips are red with provocation and the blood of her victims. She is all health and all disease. She is a masque of the red death, a Medusa who turns men to stone but the mother who stirs the blood pudding of her sons until their bodies congeal in her womb. To give life is to kill. Perhaps this *is* heaven's mother, who comes when called. She is the vampire who haunts men's dreams. Aubrey Beardsley depicts a Coleridgean epiphany of the vampire Madonna in "The Ascension of St. Rose of Lima." Here Mary hovers in the air like a poison black cloud and embraces St. Rose with lascivious thirst. The motif of monstrous epiphany also appears in Ingmar Bergman's *Through a Glass Darkly* (1961), where a mad girl waits for God to show himself. He appears as a frightful spider, menacing and sexually aggressive.

The Ancient Mariner surges forward on its wave of daemonic vision from parts 1 through 4, but then something happens to the poem. Parts 5 through 7 are a muddle. The poem recovers only when the Mariner's tale ceases and the outer narrative frame resumes where the Mariner delays the Wedding-Guest at the Bridegroom's door. *The Ancient Mariner* drags on pointlessly for too long, and I think I know where and why it begins to go wrong. At the end of part 4 the Mariner sees water snakes in the sea:

> Blue, glossy green, and velvet black,
> They coiled and swam; and every track
> Was a flash of golden fire.

This is one of the great moments in Romantic poetry. We are back at the dawn of time. Firmament has not yet separated from the waters. The sun is only a yolky yellow in the albuminous jelly of the mother-stuff. Primeval ocean swarms with slimy life. But it is also man's body shot with veins. These serpents, writhing with Vergilian opalescence, are the chains which bind us, our physical life. Man is a Laocoön bedeviled by serpents. We all struggle in the toils of our mother-born body. Why are the sea snakes veins? Because as I said, all great lines in *The Ancient Mariner* look forward to "Christabel," where the vampire has exquisite "blue-veined feet." Geraldine, the green snake who strangles the dove, is the daemon of chthonian nature, trampling man in her triumph of the will.

Coleridge has penetrated far into the daemonic realm. Too far, for there is an immediate retreat into conventional emotion. Now Coleridge's vision fails, and the poem begins to drift vaguely. Why? What have the sea snakes roused which Coleridge cannot face? The Mariner's response to them is embarrassingly simplistic. "A spring of love" gushes from his heart; he blesses them; the moment he can pray, the albatross falls from his neck and into the sea. How dreadful it is to see our shaman-poet unmasked, cranking the bellows of afflatus like a stagehand. Coleridge here has been overcome by anxiety and surrenders to Wordsworth and to Christianity. Love and prayer are a ludicrously inadequate response to the chthonian horror which Coleridge has summoned from the dark heart of existence. The roiling sea snakes are the barbaric energy of matter, the undulating spiral of birth and death. What should the proper response be to this ecstatic hallucination? Coleridge is hemmed in. His protagonist, the Mariner, is insufficiently advanced as a sexual persona. The male heroine will need to be revised if daemonic vision is to be sustained. "Christabel" is a rewriting of *The Ancient Mariner* in new and more daring terms. There, as we shall see, when the protagonist meets the serpent face of nature, there will be no swerving away. The poet, disguised so that Wordsworth can no longer find him, will hurl himself into the chthonian abyss.

The problem with moral or Christian readings of *The Ancient Mariner* is that they can make no sense of the compulsive or delusional frame of the poem. If the "spring of love" felt by the Mariner were imaginatively efficacious, the poem should be able to conclude. Or at the very least it should permit the Mariner to be redeemed. But the falling off of the albatross is followed by three more sections. And even at the end of the poem the Mariner is still forced to wander the world, repeating his "ghastly tale" again and again. Having introduced a benevolent emotion into his daemonic poem, Coleridge is at a loss how to proceed. A new cast of characters is hustled in—seraphs, a Pilot, a Hermit. There is confused dialogue, a fuzzy twisting and turning. Here is the point: the moment the Mariner prays, the moment good rather than evil triumphs, the poem falls apart. At the end of part 4 Coleridge is overwhelmed with fear at what he has written and vainly attempts to turn his poem in a redemptive direction. The superego acts to obscure what has come from the amoral id. Nineteen years later, Coleridge added the marginal glosses which still adorn the poem. These dithery festoons are afterthoughts, revisions. They often differ crucially in tone from the text which they "explain." We hear in them the Christian Coleridge trying to soften the daemonic Coleridge, exactly as the older and Urizenic Wordsworth "corrected" his early and greatest nature poetry. Rationalization and moralization are the techniques by which Coleridge strove to put out the daemonic fires of his own imagination.

The poetic discordancies are blatant in the conclusion. The Mariner says:

> O Wedding-Guest! this soul hath been
> Alone on a wide wide sea:
> So lonely 'twas, that God himself
> Scarce seeméd there to be.

This is the truth. In the cosmos of *The Ancient Mariner* Jehovah has been obliterated by the vampire mother who rises up from the slime of nature. But the Christian Coleridge keeps stitching the veil he has rent. The Mariner illogically goes on to celebrate communal churchgoing under the kind gaze of the "great Father" and ends his message thus:

> He prayeth best, who loveth best
> All things both great and small;
> For the dear God who loveth us,
> He made and loveth all.

What a frail twig to cling to in the maelstrom which is chthonian nature. One thinks of the ironically sentimental moral tags of Blake, evasive distortions of the severity of experience represented in the poems: "So if all do their duty, they need not fear harm"; "Then cherish pity, lest you drive an angel from your door." The Mariner's farewell stanzas are a poetic non sequitur. They contradict everything that is great in the poem. Coleridge himself seems to have sensed this, for long afterward he remarked that *The Ancient Mariner* had "too much" of a moral in it: "the only or chief fault, if I might say so, was the obtrusion of the moral sentiment so openly on the reader."

Imagination has the last word anyhow in *The Ancient Mariner*. Here are the closing lines, as the Wedding-Guest turns away from the door of the Bridegroom:

> He went like one that hath been stunned,
> And is of sense forlorn:
> A sadder and a wiser man,
> He rose the morrow morn.

If one accepts the Christian interpretation of the poem, how explain this peculiar reaction? The Wedding-Guest is not morally strengthened by the Mariner's exhortations. He is plunged into gloom and severed from society. The Mariner counsels Christian love, but the Wedding-Guest walks away as if the Mariner had said, "There is no God, and nature is a hell of appetite and force." But that is the secret message which the Wedding-Guest has divined, the message which has slipped past Coleridge despite his vigorous efforts to steer the poem in a morally acceptable direction. The guest arises the next day "a sadder and wiser man" because through the smokescreen of the Christian finale has come the terrible revelation of Coleridge's daemonic dream-vision.

Chronology

1772   Samuel Taylor Coleridge born in the vicarage at Ottery, St. Mary, Devonshire, on October 21.

1775   Begins formal schooling at Dame Key's Reading School.

1778   Attends Henry VIII Free Grammar School.

1781   His father, John Coleridge, dies.

1782   Admitted to Christ's Hospital School in July.

1791   Enters Jesus College, Cambridge, in July.

1793   Enlists in the King's Regiment, 15th Light Dragoons, under the pseudonym Silas Tomkyn Comberback.

1794   Obtains a discharge from the King's Regiment and returns to Cambridge. Meets Southey at Oxford. *The Fall of Robespierre* published (with Southey) under Coleridge's name. Meets Godwin. Leaves Cambridge in December, without a degree, in order to pursue the scheme of Pantisocracy.

1795   Moves to Bristol in January and meets William Wordsworth. Marries Sara Fricker of Bristol; they settle at Clevedon, Somerset. Lectures in Bristol through November on politics and history.

1796   Hartley Coleridge born. Publishes *Poems on Various Subjects* and edits the March–May issues of *The Watchman*. Moves with family to Nether Stowey.

1797   The Wordsworths move to Alfoxden to be near Coleridge. Composes *The Rime of the Ancient Mariner* and publishes *Poems* by himself, Charles Lamb, and Charles Lloyd.

1798   A second son, Berkeley, born, who later dies. Josiah and Thomas Wedgwood settle a lifetime annuity of £150 on Coleridge. Writes part 1 of "Christabel," "Frost at Midnight," "France: An Ode," "Fears in Solitude," and (?) "Kubla Khan." In September the first edition of *Lyrical Ballads* is published anonymously with Words-

	worth, while they are traveling through Germany with Dorothy Wordsworth and John Chester.
1799	Enters the University of Göttingen, alone, in February. Returns to England in July and contributes to the *Morning Post*. Meets Sara Hutchinson.
1800	Settles with family at Greta Hall, Keswick, where Derwent is born. Finishes translation of Schiller's *Wallenstein* in late spring. Second edition of *Lyrical Ballads* published with a preface by Wordsworth.
1802	The Southeys move to Greta Hall. Sara Coleridge born. Writes "Dejection: An Ode." Third edition of *Lyrical Ballads*.
1803	Abandons a tour of Scotland with William and Dorothy Wordsworth.
1804	In May leaves for Rome and Malta, having decided to separate from his wife, and with hopes that the climate will be good for his health, which has been weakened by rheumatism and opium addiction.
1806	Returns to England by way of Italy. Separates from his wife.
1807	De Quincey meets Coleridge in Somerset.
1808	January–June gives his first series of lectures, on "Principles of Poetry," at the Royal Institution in London. Later is guest, along with De Quincey, at the Wordsworth home at Grasmere.
1809	Begins *The Friend*. Contributions to *The Courier* to 1817.
1810	*The Friend* ended. Leaves the Lake District for London and breaks with Wordsworth.
1811	Lectures on the English poets in London. Josiah Wedgwood withdraws his half of the legacy.
1812	Lectures in London and Bristol. Makes up with Wordsworth.
1813	Early play *Osorio*, revised as *Remorse*, performed at Drury Lane Theatre in London.
1814	Stays with his friend John Morgan in London and Calne, Wiltshire.
1815	Begins dictating *Biographia Literaria* in Calne. Health declining.
1816	Stays at Highgate, London, as patient of Dr. James Gillman. In June publishes a volume of poetry containing "Christabel," "Kubla Khan," and "The Pains of Sleep." Also brings out *The Statesman's Manual: or The Bible the Best Guide to Political Skill and Foresight*.
1817	Publishes *Biographia Literaria*, *Sibylline Leaves*, and his two *Lay Sermons*.

1818   Lectures on English poetry and history of philosophy. Publishes a selection from *The Friend* and *On Method*, a preliminary treatise to the *Encyclopaedia Metropolitana*.

1819   Ends lectures on history of philosophy.

1825   May–June publishes *Aids to Reflection in the Formation of a Manly Character*.

1828   *Poetical Works* published. Tours Germany with Wordsworth.

1830   *On the Constitution of Church and State* published.

1834   Dies on July 25 at Gillman residence, Highgate.

1836   Four volumes of Coleridge's *Literary Remains* edited by Henry Nelson Coleridge.

1840   *Confessions of an Enquiring Spirit* published.

Contributors

HAROLD BLOOM, Sterling Professor of the Humanities at Yale University, is the author of *The Anxiety of Influence*, *Poetry and Repression*, and many other volumes of literary criticism. His forthcoming study, *Freud: Transference and Authority*, attempts a full-scale reading of all Freud's major writings. A MacArthur Prize Fellow, he is general editor of five series of literary criticism published by Chelsea House.

ELLIOTT B. GOSE, JR., is Professor of English at the University of British Columbia. He is the author of *Imagination Indulged: The Irrational in the Nineteenth-Century English Novel* and *The Transformation Process in Joyce's Ulysses*.

WILLIAM EMPSON, a prominent poet and literary critic, became Professor of English at Sheffield University after teaching at several universities in China and Japan. His critical works include: *Seven Types of Ambiguity*, *Some Versions of the Pastoral*, *The Structure of Complex Words*, and *Milton's God*.

GEOFFREY H. HARTMAN is Karl Young Professor of Comparative Literature at Yale. His influential work in critical theory includes *Blindness and Insight* and *Allegories of Reading*.

WARREN STEVENSON is the author of *Divine Analogy: A Study of the Creation Motif in Blake and Coleridge* and *The Myth of the Golden Age in English Romantic Poetry*.

FRANCES FERGUSON is Professor of English at the University of California, Berkeley. Her writings on Romanticism and the Sublime include her book, *Wordsworth: Language as Counter-Spirit*.

LAWRENCE LIPKING is Chester Tripp Professor of Humanities and English at Northwestern University. A Guggenheim fellow, he is the author of

The Ordering of the Arts in Eighteenth-Century England, The Life of the Poet, and many other critical studies.

LESLIE BRISMAN is Professor of English at Yale, and the author of *Milton's Poetry of Choice and Its Romantic Heirs* and *Romantic Origins.*

CAMILLE PAGLIA teaches at the Philadelphia College of the Performing Arts and is the author of the forthcoming *Sexual Personae,* a study of sexual identities in Western literature and art.

Bibliography

Bald, R. C. "Coleridge and *The Ancient Mariner*: Addenda to *The Road to Xanadu*." In *Nineteenth Century Studies*, edited by Herbert Davis, William C. DeVane, and R. C. Bald, 1–45. Ithaca, N. Y.: Cornell University Press, 1940.

Bate, Walter Jackson. "*The Ancient Mariner*." In *Coleridge*, 55–65. New York: The Macmillan Co., 1968.

Beer, John. "The Glorius Sun." In *Coleridge the Visionary*, 133–74. London: Chatto & Windus, 1977.

Bellis, George. "The Fixed Crime of *The Ancient Mariner*." *Essays in Criticism* 24 (1974): 243–60.

Beres, David. "A Dream, a Vision, and a Poem: A Psychoanalytic Study of *The Rime of the Ancient Mariner*." *The International Journal of Psychoanalysis* 32 (1951): 97–116.

Bodkin, Maud. "A Study of *The Ancient Mariner* and of the Rebirth Archetype." In *Archetypal Patterns in Poetry: Psychological Studies of Imagination*, 26–88. London: Oxford University Press, 1934.

Bostetter, Edward E. "The Nightmare World of *The Ancient Mariner*." *Studies in Romanticism* 1 (1962): 241–54.

Boulger, James D. "Christian Skepticism in *The Rime of the Ancient Mariner*." In *From Sensibility to Romanticism*, edited by Frederick W. Hilles and Harold Bloom, 439–52. New York: Oxford University Press, 1965.

————, ed. *Twentieth Century Interpretations of "The Rime of the Ancient Mariner."* Englewood Cliffs, N. J.: Prentice-Hall, 1969.

Bowra, C. M. "*The Ancient Mariner*." In *The Romantic Imagination*, 51–75. New York: Oxford University Press, 1961.

Brett, R. L. *Reason and Imagination: A Study of Form and Meaning in Four Poems.* New York: Oxford University Press for the University of Hull, 1960.

Buchan, A. M. "The Sad Wisdom of the Mariner." *Studies in Philology* 61 (1964): 669–88.

Burke, Kenneth. "*The Ancient Mariner*." In *The Philosophy of Literary Form*. Berkeley: University of California Press, 1974.

Chayes, Irene H. "A Coleridgean Reading of *The Ancient Mariner*." *Studies in Romanticism* 25 (1965): 81–103.

D'Avanzo, Mario L. "Coleridge's Wedding Guest and Marriage Feast: The Biblical Context." *University of Windsor Review* 8 (1972): 62–65.

———. "Her Looks Were Free: The Ancient Mariner and the Harlot." *English Language Notes* 17 (1980): 185–89.

Delson, Abe. "A Search for Meaning: A Critical History of the Thematic Interpretations of *The Rime of the Ancient Mariner*." *Dissertation Abstracts International* (1970): 4447A–48A.

———. "The Symbolism of the Sun and the Moon in *The Rime of the Ancient Mariner*." *Texas Studies in Literature and Language* 15 (1974): 707–720.

Dyck, Sarah. "Perspective in *The Rime of the Ancient Mariner*." *Studies in English Literature* 13 (1973): 591–604.

Empson, William, and David Pirie, eds. *Coleridge's Verse: A Selection*. London: Faber & Faber, 1972.

Fogle, Richard Harter. "The Genre of *The Ancient Mariner*." *Texas Studies in English Literature* 7 (1957): 111–24.

Forstner, Lorne J. "Coleridge's *The Ancient Mariner* and the Case for Justifiable 'Mythocide': An Argument on Psychological, Epistemological, and Formal Grounds." *Criticism* 18 (1976): 211–29.

Fulmer, O. Bryan. "*The Ancient Mariner* and the *Wandering Jew*." *Studies in Philology* 66 (1969): 797–815.

Gardner, W. H. "The Poet and the Albatross (A Study in Symbolic Suggestion)." *English Studies in Africa* 1 (1958): 102–25.

Harding, D. C. W. "The Theme of *The Ancient Mariner*." *Scrutiny* 9 (1941): 334–42.

Haven, Richard. "*The Ancient Mariner* in the Nineteenth Century." *Studies in Romanticism* 11 (1972): 360–74.

———. *Patterns of Consciousness: An Essay on Coleridge*. Amherst: The University of Massachusetts Press, 1969.

House, Humphry. *The Clark Lectures 1951–52*. London: Rupert Hart-Davis, 1953.

Jackson, J. R. de J., ed. *Coleridge: The Critical Heritage*. London: Routledge & Kegan Paul, 1969.

Knight, G. W. "*The Rime of the Ancient Mariner*." In *The Starlit Dome: Studies in the Poetry of Vision*. London: Oxford University Press, 1971.

Lowes, John Livingston. *The Road to Xanadu*. Boston: Houghton Mifflin Co., 1927.

McDonald, Daniel. "Too Much Reality: A Discussion of *The Rime of the Ancient Mariner*." *Studies in English Literature* 4 (1964): 543–54.

McGann, Jerome, Jr. "The Meaning of *The Ancient Mariner*." *Critical Inquiry* 8 (1981): 35–67.

McLuhan, Marshall. "Coleridge as Artist." In *The Literary Criticism of Marshall McLuhan 1943–1962*, edited by Eugene McNamara. New York: McGraw-Hill Book Company, 1969.

Magnuson, Paul. *Coleridge's Nightmare Poetry*. Charlottesville: University of Virginia Press, 1974.

Mileur, Jean-Pierre. "The Prophetic Reader and the Psychologically Contingent: The Mystery Poems." In *Vision and Revision: Coleridge's Art of Immanence*, 61–89. Berkeley: University of California Press, 1982.

Modiano, Raimonda. "Words and 'Languageless' Meanings: Limits of Expression in *The Rime of the Ancient Mariner*." *Modern Language Quarterly* 38 (1977): 40–77.

Owen, Charles A., Jr. "Structure in *The Ancient Mariner*." *College English* 23 (1962): 261–67.

Payne, Richard. " 'The Style and Spirit of the Elder Poets': *The Ancient Mariner* and English Literary Tradition." *Modern Philology* 75 (1978): 369–84.

Piper, H. W. "*The Ancient Mariner*: Biblical Allegory, Poetic Symbolism and Religious Crisis." *Southern Review* 10 (1977): 232–42.

Pottle, Frederick. "Modern Criticism of *The Ancient Mariner*." In *Essays on the Teaching of English*. New York: Appleton-Century-Crofts, 1960.

Reed, Arden. "The Riming Mariner and the Mariner Rimed." In *Romantic Weather*: *The Climates of Coleridge and Baudelaire*, 147–81. Providence, R. I.: University Press of New England for Brown University Press, 1983.

Richards, I. A. "Coleridge: The Vulnerable Poet." *Yale Review* 48 (1959): 491–504.

Schultz, Max F. "The Ventriloquism Voice." In *The Poetic Voices of Coleridge*, 51–71. Detroit: Wayne State University Press, 1964.

Sitterson, Joseph C., Jr. "*The Rime of the Ancient Mariner* and Freudian Dream Theory." *Papers on Language and Literature* 18 (1982): 17–35.

Stevenson, Lionel. "*The Ancient Mariner* as a Dramatic Monologue." *Personalist* 30 (1949): 34–44.

Tillyard, E. M. W. "Coleridge: *The Rime of the Ancient Mariner*." In *Poetry and Its Background: Illustrated by Five Poems 1470–1870*, 66–86. New York: Barnes & Noble, 1970.

Twitchell, James. "*The Rime of the Ancient Mariner* as Vampire Poem." *College Literature* 4 (1977): 21–39.

Vlasopolos, Anca. "Symbol as Translucence." In *The Symbolic Method of Coleridge, Baudelaire and Yeats*, 71–112. Detroit: Wayne State University Press, 1983.

Warren, Robert Penn. "A Poem of Pure Imagination: An Experiment in Reading." In *The Rime of the Ancient Mariner*, by Samuel Taylor Coleridge, 61–148. New York: Reynal & Hitchcock, 1946.

Whalley, George. "The Mariner and the Albatross." *The University of Toronto Quarterly* 16 (1947): 381–98.

Acknowledgments

Introduction (originally entitled " 'Natural Magic': *The Ancient Mariner*") by Harold Bloom from *The Visionary Company* by Harold Bloom, © 1971 by Cornell University Press. Reprinted by permission of the publisher.

"Coleridge and the Luminous Gloom: An Analysis of the 'Symbolical Language' in *The Rime of the Ancient Mariner*" by Elliott B. Gose, Jr., from *PMLA* 75, no. 3 (June 1960), © 1960 by the Modern Language Association of America. Reprinted by permission of the Modern Language Association.

"The Ancient Mariner" by William Empson from *Critical Quarterly* 6, no. 4 (Winter 1964), © 1964 by Sir William Empson. Reprinted by permission of Lady Hetta Empson.

"Representation in *The Ancient Mariner*" (originally entitled "From 'Salisbury Plain' to 'The Ruined Cottage' ") by Geoffrey H. Hartman from *Wordsworth's Poetry 1787–1814* by Geoffrey H. Hartman, © 1964 and 1971 by Yale University. Reprinted by permission of Yale University Press. The second and third parts of this essay (originally entitled "Christopher Smart's *Magnificat*" and "Evening Star and Evening Land") are taken from *The Fate of Reading* by Geoffrey H. Hartman, © 1975 by The University of Chicago. Reprinted by permission of The University of Chicago Press.

"*The Rime of the Ancient Mariner* as Epic Symbol" by Warren Stevenson from *Dalhousie Review* 56, no. 3 (Autumn 1976), © 1976 by Dalhousie University Press. Reprinted by permission.

"Coleridge and the Deluded Reader: *The Rime of the Ancient Mariner*" by Frances Ferguson from *Georgia Review* 31, no. 3 (Fall 1977), © 1977 by The University of Georgia. Reprinted by permission of *The Georgia Review* and Frances Ferguson.

"The Marginal Gloss" by Lawrence Lipking from *Critical Inquiry* 3, no. 4 (Summer 1977), © 1977 by The University of Chicago. Reprinted by permission of The University of Chicago Press.

"Coleridge and the Ancestral Voices" by Leslie Brisman from *Romantic Origins* by

Index

821.7--S
Samuel Taylor Coleridge's The
rime of the ancient mariner

821.7--S
Samuel Taylor Coleridge's The rime of
the ancient mariner

Rockingham Public Library

Harrisonburg, Virginia   22801

1. Books may be kept two weeks and may be renewed twice for the same period, unless reserved.

2. A fine is charged for each day a book is not returned according to the above rule. No book will be issued to any person incurring such a fine until it has been paid.

3. All injuries to books beyond reasonable wear and all losses shall be made good to the satisfaction of the Librarian.

4. Each borrower is held responsible for all books charged on his card and for all fines accruing on the same.